Best Easy Day Hikes
Camden

Help Us Keep This Guide Up to Date

Every effort has been made by the author and editors to make this guide as accurate and useful as possible. However, many things can change after a guide is published—trails are rerouted, regulations change, facilities come under new management, and so forth.

We appreciate hearing from you concerning your experiences with this guide and how you feel it could be improved and kept up to date. While we may not be able to respond to all comments and suggestions, we'll take them to heart, and we'll also make certain to share them with the author. Please send your comments and suggestions to the following address:

Globe Pequot Press
Reader Response/Editorial Department
246 Goose Lane
Guilford, CT 06437

Or you may e-mail us at:

editorial@falcon.com

Thanks for your input, and happy trails!

Best Easy Day Hikes Series

Best Easy Day Hikes
Camden

Greg Westrich

FALCONGUIDES

GUILFORD, CONNECTICUT
HELENA, MONTANA

FALCONGUIDES®

An imprint of Rowman & Littlefield
Falcon, FalconGuides, and Outfit Your Mind are registered trademarks
of Rowman & Littlefield.

Distributed by NATIONAL BOOK NETWORK

Copyright © 2015 by Rowman & Littlefield
Maps: Alena Pearce © Rowman & Littlefield

British Library Cataloguing-in-Publication Information available

Library of Congress Cataloging-in-Publication Data available

ISBN 978-1-4930-1000-4 (paperback)
ISBN 978-1-4930-1474-3 (ebook)

∞™ The paper used in this publication meets the minimum require-
ments of American National Standard for Information Sciences—
Permanence of Paper for Printed Library Materials, ANSI/NISO
Z39.48-1992.

Contents

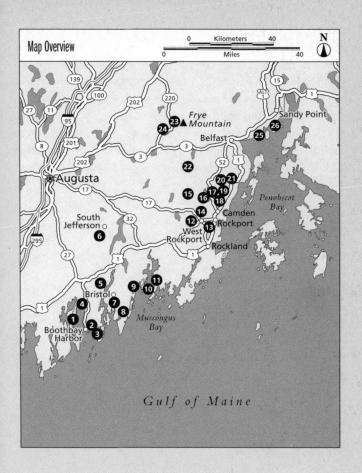

Kilometers

Miles

N

139

100

11

27

95

220

Frye
Mountain

23

24

Sandy Point

25

26

202

202

8

201

3

Belfast

3

52

1

Augusta

22

17

20 21

17 19

15

16 18

South
Jefferson

32

14

Camden

Penobscot
Bay

6

12

Rockport

295

27

13

West
Rockport

Rockland

1

1

5

11

Bristol

9

10

4

7

8

Muscongus
Bay

1

2

3

Boothbay
Harbor

Gulf of Maine

Acknowledgments

This guide would not be possible without the hard work and dedication of the people who work to protect Maine's natural places and build the trails we all love and use.

I owe a special thanks to my wife, Ann, and my two children, Henry and Emma. Without their support and help, this guide would have never happened. Most of these hikes were completed as a family.

Introduction

Maine's Mid-Coast is one of the most convoluted coastlines in the United States. Hundreds of miles of shoreline are packed into a compact arch of coast between the mouths of the Kennebec and Penobscot Rivers. The region is characterized by long, narrow peninsulas and islands bounded by equally narrow bays—often called rivers. This landscape is a result of the underlying bedrock. The Mid-Coast's bedrock is mostly deformed sedimentary rock—especially shales—that have been folded and stacked on end, perpendicular to the coastline. The dips in the bedding form the bays; the high points the peninsulas. The tectonic action that deformed the Mid-Coast's bedrock also injected other minerals, such as granite, into the gaps. The result is a coastline that is interesting and varied.

The few sand beaches occur where tidal action has sorted the debris and deposited large amounts of sand carried out into the Gulf of Maine by the region's rivers. Most of the shoreline is either broken bedrock or cobbles.

The first settlers to Camden arrived as early as 1768, when General Samuel Waldo—for whom Waldo County to the north is named—was given title to the land by the English Lord Chancellor, 1st Earl, Lord Camden, Charles Pratt, who Waldo judiciously named the town after. Camden grew into an important manufacturing and shipbuilding town. Camden was later eclipsed by Rockland during that town's granite boom. Today both towns are bustling tourist destinations with shops and galleries. Camden has been called the prettiest town in America.

Inland, the Mid-Coast was settled by fiercely independent folks who named their towns not after where they came from or British lords, but after ideals like Freedom, Unity,

Hope, Union, and Liberty. Their ancestors, along with a good number of refugees from southern New England's urban centers, lived quiet, rural lives among rolling hills and hardwood forests. Quite different from the towns along US 1.

Where the coastline bends north to form the western side of Penobscot Bay, the shore becomes less convoluted because the bedrock is parallel to the coastline. Behind the coast from Rockland to Belfast are low, rugged mountains. Even though many of the coastal towns of Penobscot Bay were built around quarrying granite, these mountains are not granite. The granite that made the Mid-Coast rich was quarried from the islands on the east side of Penobscot Bay. You can tell which islands are granite and which are not by looking at a map: The round islands are granite; the elongated or irregular islands are not.

The Camden Hills, and the other mountains of the region, are close to the coast, offering fine views from their rocky flanks and summits. Camden Hills State Park contains many of these mountains, but just as many are scattered south and west along the coast. The town of Camden owns a small ski area on the northeast flank of Ragged Mountain that is the only ski resort in the country with a view of the Atlantic Ocean.

This guide contains hikes across this varied landscapes within an hour's drive of Camden: the busy mountains of Camden Hills State Park, the site of a colonial fort at the mouth of the Penobscot River, rocky coastline where eagles and osprey soar, forests where blueberries abound on low granite ledges, remote mountains rarely climbed, and oak-pine forests right down to cobbled beaches.

Wildlife

By weight there are more salamanders in Maine than moose, which is another way to say that most wildlife isn't big, but small. You won't see any large mammals hiking near Camden, but you will—if you look around—see plenty of wildlife. There are moose, coyotes, and bears living near Camden, especially inland, but they are far less common than in the North Woods.

Dozens of species of amphibians are out there for you to find. It's not uncommon to see a half dozen different kinds of frogs and toads on a hike. Maine also has several kinds of snakes—none poisonous—that often sun on warm trails.

Maine is also home to numerous weasels and rodents. You are unlikely to see a stoat or fisher, but you would be hard-pressed to take a hike free of squirrels. They sit on downfall or in trees, commenting loudly on passing hikers. Beavers are common in Maine's lakes and streams. Their handiwork is easy to find, but seeing one of the shy rodents is less common. They are most active in the twilight of early morning and late evening. Be on the lookout for porcupines. During the day they often can be found sleeping in trees near where they've been feeding.

Maine's coast is a magnet for birders because of the diverse habitats and the presence of northern species not found elsewhere in the United States. Birdsong is a constant presence on hikes, whether it's the chatter of a family of chickadees, the musical song of a hermit thrush, or the cry of circling osprey. Your ears will find many more birds than your eyes. A few of the hikes in this guide pass very near active osprey nests. The best birding is during spring and fall migrations, but the coast offers sea birds and ducks that come from the north for the relatively milder climate and protected waters along the Mid-Coast.

Bugs

One theory holds that Maine is so sparsely populated because of the biting insects. They can be quite annoying—even ruin an otherwise great day of hiking. There are black-flies, checker flies, moose flies, no-see-ums, mosquitoes, and, recently, ticks. Blackflies are worst between Mother's Day and Father's Day, but are around all summer. They are only active during the day. Blackfly saliva numbs your skin, so you often aren't aware of all your bites until they start bleeding and itching. Over time their bites seem to cause less swelling and itching, as if the immune system learns to fight back. Even so, when these pests are at their worst, many Mainers wear a bug net over their head for protection.

Mosquitoes are active day and night and are most common in cool, damp areas. This means that unless there's snow on the ground, there is something out there that wants to bite you. Always carry bug dope. Having said that, you will have many bug-free hiking days, especially when it's breezy.

In 2013, when I hiked 800 miles for *Hiking Maine*, I got exactly one tick. In 2014 I hiked less than 200 miles for *Best Easy Day Hikes Camden* and got too many ticks to count. On one hike—that didn't make the book—I removed more than 40 ticks from my legs. Ticks are most common in tall grass. After hiking through a meadow or open area, you should check yourself for ticks and remove them before they get a chance to attach.

Plant Life

Tourists flock to New England in the fall for the foliage, and it's well worth the trip. But what many people—even native Mainers—miss are the spring colors. When the trees begin to leaf out, the mountainsides are awash in varying shades of green with reds and yellows thrown in. Maybe it's not as dramatic as in the fall, but beautiful just the same. Beneath the trees a profusion of wildflowers rush to bloom before the canopy closes and leaves them in the shade for the summer.

Through the summer, a succession of berries ripens for hikers to snack on. Especially prized are blueberries. Good blueberry spots are noted in this guide. The blueberries usually begin to ripen in mid- to late July. When you're suffering through the blackflies early in the summer, remember them as you are munching on trailside blueberries: Blackflies are an important blueberry pollinator.

In the fall, beneath the vibrant trees, there is an explosion of mushrooms. At least a thousand varieties of fungi are native to Maine. Most of the time they live unobserved within the soil, in rotting vegetation, and on tree roots. But in the fall they bloom: Fungi send up fruiting bodies that release spoors—like tiny seeds—into the air. We call these fruiting bodies mushrooms.

Weather and Seasons

You hear a lot of Mainers say that if you don't like the weather, wait five minutes and it'll change. Of course, that's an exaggeration, but not by much. On any given day the weather across the state can vary widely. In general it's cooler, milder, and breezier along the coast. The Maine coast is among the foggiest places on Earth, but don't let that keep you off the trails. Hiking in fog can be a wonderful experience. In winter, when most of the state is buried under deep snow, you can hike near the coast. You just have to be careful of ice. Often the milder weather along the coast leaves trails sheened with ice instead of snow.

Many of the hikes in this book are inaccessible in winter. Before you head out, check the individual trail description for access. Hiking in the winter—with or without snowshoes—can be extra work, but is often worth the effort. Maine in winter offers great solitude and beautiful landscapes.

Spring is mud season in Maine. Trails are often muddy and wet. Still, spring hiking is wonderful. Wildflowers are beginning to emerge, the birds are singing, and there are no bugs yet.

Summer more than triples the population of Maine. There are more summer homes here than in any other state. Most of the tourists and summer people congregate along the coast and in the towns, especially after July 4. Most of the hikes never get crowded. Even when downtown Camden has bumper-to-bumper traffic, you can find solitude on a hike most days. It rarely gets hotter than the mid-80s, but you still need to be prepared for hot, dry conditions in summer.

Fall can be the best time for hiking: The summer crowds are gone, the weather is cooler, and after the first freeze the bugs are gone. And then there are the fall colors. Most years you can hike right up until around Thanksgiving without having to worry much about snow. It can and does snow as early as late September, though, so bring appropriate clothing and gear.

To be safe, no matter what the season or the weather when you start a hike, assume it will change. Always bring a jacket and raincoat, even on the warmest summer day. In spring and fall it's best to layer, so you can put on and take off layers as needed. Remember: It's best to start out cool; sweat is the enemy. Except in summer, avoid cotton clothes. Cotton is comfortable, but when it gets wet or sweaty it can be cold, even dangerously so. Adding a few things to your pack just in case may make the climbs a little tougher, but in the long run it will make your hikes safer and more comfortable. Maine's weather is not something to complain about; rather it's something to prepare for and then enjoy in all its various manifestations. The bottom line: Each season and every kind of weather in Maine can make for great hiking.

Be Prepared

Hiking around Camden is generally safe. Still, hikers should be prepared. Here is some specific advice:

- Know the basics of first aid, including how to treat bleeding, bites and stings, and fractures, strains, and sprains. Pack a first-aid kit on every excursion.

- Familiarize yourself with the symptoms of heat exhaustion and heatstroke. Heat exhaustion symptoms include heavy sweating, muscle cramps, headache, dizziness, and fainting. Should you or any of your hiking party exhibit any of these symptoms, cool the victim down immediately by rehydrating and getting him or her to an air-conditioned location. Cold showers also help reduce body temperature. Heatstroke is much more serious: The victim may lose consciousness, and the skin is hot and dry to the touch. In this event call 911 immediately.

- Regardless of the weather, your body needs a lot of water while hiking. A full 32-ounce bottle is the minimum for these short hikes, but more is always better. Bring a full water bottle, whether water is available along the trail or not.

- Don't drink from streams, rivers, creeks, or lakes without treating or filtering the water first. Waterways and water bodies may host a variety of contaminants, including giardia, which can cause serious intestinal unrest.

- Prepare for extremes of both heat and cold by dressing in layers.

- Carry a backpack in which you can store extra clothing, ample drinking water and food, and whatever goodies, like guidebooks, cameras, and binoculars, you might want. Consider bringing a GPS with tracking capabilities or enable the GPS function on your phone.

- Cell phone coverage is generally good, but you can never be absolutely sure until you are on location. Bring your device, but make sure you've turned it off or got it on the vibrate setting while hiking. Nothing like a "wake the dead"–loud ring to startle every creature on the trail, including fellow hikers.

- Keep children under careful watch. Trails travel along cliffs and beside lakes and streams, most of which are not recommended for swimming. Be watchful along designated overlooks. Hazards along some of the trails include poison ivy, uneven footing, and steep drop-offs; make sure children do not stray from the designated route. Children should carry a plastic whistle; if they become lost, they should stay in one place and blow the whistle to summon help.

Leave No Trace

Trails in Camden are well used during spring, summer, and fall—the hiking season. As trail users, we must be especially vigilant to make sure our passage leaves no lasting mark. Here are some basic guidelines for preserving trails in the region:

- Pack out all your own trash, including biodegradable items like orange peels. You might also pack out garbage left by less-considerate hikers.
- Don't approach or feed any wild creatures—the ground squirrel eyeing your snack food is best able to survive if it remains self-reliant.
- Don't pick wildflowers or gather rocks, antlers, feathers, or other treasures along the trail, especially historic relics. Removing these items will only take away from the next hiker's experience and steal a piece of the historic puzzle found in area parks.
- Avoid damaging trailside soils and prairie plants by remaining on the established route. This is also a good rule of thumb for avoiding poison ivy and other common regional trailside irritants.
- Be courteous by not making loud noises while hiking.
- Some of these trails are multiuse, which means you'll share them with other hikers, trail runners, mountain bikers, and equestrians. Familiarize yourself with the proper trail etiquette, yielding the trail when appropriate.
- Use outhouses at trailheads or along the trail.

For more information, visit LNT.org.

How to Use This Guide

To aid in quick decision making, each hike chapter begins with a hike summary. These short summaries give you a taste of the hiking adventure to follow. Next you'll find the quick, nitty-gritty details of the hike: location of the trailhead, hike's distance, hiking time, difficulty rating, best season to take the hike, trail surface, land status, nearest town, other trail users you may encounter, water availability, canine compatability, fee and/or permit information, where to find maps, and trail contacts (for updates on trail conditions). The Finding the Trailhead section gives you dependable directions from downtown Camden, right down to where you'll want to park your car. The hike description is the meat of the chapter, where you'll get a more detailed description of the trail. In Miles and Directions, mileage cues identify all turns and trail name changes, as well as points of interest.

Difficulty Ratings

These are all easy hikes, but easy is a relative term. To aid in the selection of a hike that suits particular needs and abilities, each is rated easy, moderate, or more challenging. Bear in mind that even challenging routes can be made easy by hiking within your limits and taking rests when you need them.

- **Easy** hikes are generally short and flat, taking no longer than an hour to complete.
- **Moderate** hikes involve increased distance and relatively mild changes in elevation and will take 1 to 2 hours to complete.

- **More challenging** hikes feature some steep stretches and greater distances and generally take longer than 2 hours to complete.

These are completely subjective ratings—consider that what you think is easy is entirely dependent on your level of fitness and the adequacy of your gear (primarily shoes). If you are hiking with a group, you should select a hike with a rating that is appropriate for the least fit and prepared in your party.

Approximate hiking times are based on the assumption that on flat ground, most walkers average 2 miles per hour. Adjust that rate by the steepness of the terrain and your level of fitness (subtract time if you are an aerobic animal and add time if you are hiking with kids), and you have a ballpark hiking duration. Be sure to add more time if you plan to picnic or take part in other activities like bird watching or photography.

Trail Finder

Best Hikes for Coast Lovers

1 Porter Preserve

3 Linekin Preserve

4 Ovens Mouth

5 Dodge Point

8 LaVerna Preserve

9 Hockomock Nature Trail

10 Martin Point

18 Mount Megunticook

19 Bald Rock Mountain

25 Sears Island

26 Fort Point State Park

Best Hikes for Geology Lovers

4 Ovens Mouth

5 Dodge Point

8 LaVerna Preserve

14 Ragged Mountain

15 Hatchet Mountain

16 Fernald's Neck

17 Maiden Cliff

18 Mount Megunticook

Best Hikes for Birders

1 Porter Preserve

3 Linekin Preserve

4 Ovens Mouth

5 Dodge Point

7 Crooked Farm

8 LaVerna Preserve

Best Hikes for Swimming

Best Hikes for History Lovers

Best Hikes for Children

Best Hikes for Great Views

Best Hikes for Blueberries

Best Hikes for Peak Baggers

Map Legend

═══⟨95⟩═══	Interstate Highway
═══⟨1⟩═══	US Highway
═══⟨52⟩═══	State Highway
═══════	Local Road
─ ─ ─ ─ ─	Unpaved Road
▪▪▪▪▪▪▪	Featured Trail
- - - - - -	Trail
‖‖‖‖‖‖‖‖	Boardwalk/Steps
∼∼∼	River/Creek
⬭	Body of Water
⬚	State/County/Preserve/Wilderness
▬	Bench
⏝	Bridge
✪	Capital
┃	Gate
⚡	Lighthouse
▲	Mountain/Peak
🅿	Parking
■	Point of Interest/Structure
⛨	Restrooms
⚲	Spring
⌷	Tower
○	Town
❶	Trailhead
⚑	Viewpoint/Overlook
❓	Visitor/Information Center

1 Porter Preserve

The short Porter Preserve hike on Barters Island passes through an old-growth forest to Back River. The trail follows along the shore of the river to a small sandy beach on the Sheepscot River. Along the way are several overlooks and access points to the water. All the areas of land you can see from the hike are islands as well.

Start: From the trailhead at the south end of the parking area
Distance: 1.2-mile loop
Hiking time: About 1 to 2 hours
Difficulty: Easy
Best season: Apr–Oct
Trail surface: Woodland path and exposed bedrock
Land status: Porter Preserve
Nearest town: Boothbay
Other trail users: None

Water availability: None
Canine compatibility: Dogs must be on a leash at all times
Fees and permits: No fees or permits are required
Maps: *DeLorme's The Maine Atlas and Gazetteer* map 7; *USGS Westport*
Trail contact: Boothbay Region Land Trust, (207) 633-4818, www.bbrlt.org

Finding the trailhead: From downtown Camden, drive south 39.7 miles on US 1. Turn left onto ME 27. Drive 7.8 miles to Boothbay Center. Turn right onto Corey Lane. Drive miles 0.2. Turn right onto Barters Island Road. Drive miles 2.4, passing the Coastal Maine Botanical Gardens and crossing two bridges. Turn left onto Kimball-town Road. Drive 0.5 miles. Turn left onto Porter Point Road. The parking area is ahead 0.1 miles on the right, across the lane from a cemetery. Trailhead GPS: N43 52.711' / W69 40.909'

The Hike

Across Porter Point Road from the trailhead is a picturesque cemetery surrounded by a low stone wall. Either before or after the hike, take the time to stroll among the old grave markers and shading hardwoods. The hike first passes through a forest of old-growth oak and pine, among the largest trees you'll find along the Mid-Coast.

Once to the Back River there are several short side trails that lead out to the rocky shore with fine views of the surrounding islands. All the areas of land you can see from this hike are islands, most long and narrow like Barters Island, which the preserve is on. Together these islands make up much of the land of the Boothbay and Georgetown Peninsulas. The rivers that flow between the islands are all narrow bays of salt water where the tides churn in and out twice daily.

As the trail turns north along the Sheepscot River, it comes to a small rounded cove with a sand beach. Access to the beach is on a side trail at its head or from the rocks on the north side of the cove.

North of the cove the trail crosses a rocky head beneath spreading oaks great for climbing or admiring. You can wander off the trail and down a spit of rock to the water here before following the trail inland back to the trailhead.

Miles and Directions

0.0   Begin at the white blazed trailhead at the southeast corner of the parking area.

0.1   First access to the shore of Back River.

0.3   Side trail 200 feet to shore.

0.4   Reach Porter Point.

0.6   Pass several overlooks and shore access. Reach overlook of a small cove with a sand beach.

0.7   Side trail at the back of the cove with access to the beach.

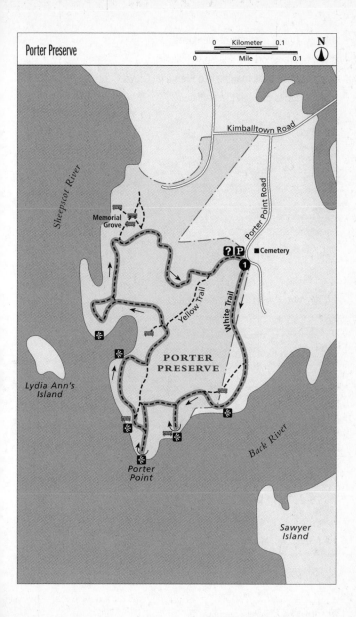

Porter Preserve

Kimballtown Road

Sheepscot River

Porter Point Road

Memorial Grove

Cemetery

Yellow Trail

White Trail

PORTER PRESERVE

Lydia Ann's Island

Porter Point

Back River

Sawyer Island

N

0   Kilometer   0.1
0   Mile   0.1

0.8	Rocky overlook of the cove.
0.9	Last shore access on the hike.
1.0	Pass trails leading into Memorial Grove.
1.2	Arrive back at the trailhead.

2 Lobster Cove Meadow

This short hike passes through several distinct ecosystems. First you descend through a mixed forest along a small stream. Then you cross a large meadow on your way to Meadow Cove Creek. The trail follows along the marshy creek, then crosses the southern edge of the meadow before passing through a sandy flat. The hike returns to the trailhead over a small hill through a pine forest with an understory of rocks, moss, and showy white wildflowers.

Start: From the trailhead to the left of the paved driveway next to the kiosk

Distance: 1.1-mile lollipop

Hiking time: About 1 to 2 hours

Difficulty: Easy

Best season: May–Oct

Trail surface: Woodland path and ATV trail

Land status: Lobster Cove Meadow Preserve

Nearest town: East Boothbay

Other trail users: Part of the hike is on an ATV trail

Water availability: None

Canine compatibility: Dogs must be on a leash at all times

Fees and permits: None

Maps: *DeLorme's The Maine Atlas and Gazetteer* map 7; *USGS Pemaquid Point*

Trail contact: Boothbay Region Land Trust, (207) 633-4818, www.bbrlt.org

Finding the trailhead: From downtown Camden, drive south 39.7 miles on US 1. Turn left onto ME 27. Drive 10.8 miles to Boothbay Harbor. Turn left onto ME 96 at the traffic light. Drive 0.6 miles. Turn right onto Eastern Avenue. Drive 0.1 miles. Turn left onto Highland Park Road and immediately turn left again onto a driveway. The parking is on the right near the kiosk. The trailhead is to the left of the paved driveway beyond the kiosk. Trailhead GPS: N43 51.695' / W69 37.032'

The Hike

The hike begins by following a hosta-lined path across someone's yard to an old woods road, a reminder that people have been using this land for generations. The woods road descends along a small stream to a large meadow. The trail crosses the meadow—once a pasture—to Meadow Cove Creek. The winding stream with marshy edges is kept full by a dam downstream, originally built to create a pond here. In winters the ice was commercially harvested and shipped to cities to the south. It was a thriving business until refrigeration. After commercial icing ended, beavers kept the valley flooded for their own purposes. Today the Boothbay Regional Land Trust maintains the dam to save the historic character of the stream.

The trail follows the stream to the southern end of the meadow, then turns west and crosses to a sandy flat. Look for birds' nests in the bushes and trees along the meadow's edge. Several kinds of butterflies flit about, visiting the many kinds of summer wildflowers that grow with the grasses.

From here south along the ATV trail, there are several old and abandoned gravel and sand pits. Most have begun to look natural. You can follow the ATV trail south to Lobster Cove Road, where the Indian Trail heads north along the other side of Meadow Cove Creek to the Appalachee Preserve.

The hike turns off the ATV trail and onto the White Trail just before one of the old gravel pits. The White Trail climbs a small hill into a forest of mature white pines. The trail wanders among the pines through rocks, moss, and showy white wildflowers, the trail spongy with fallen needles.

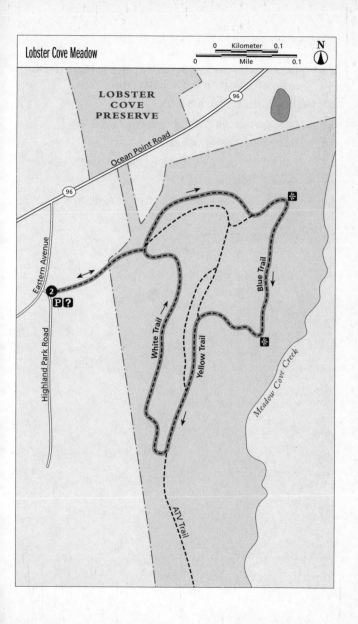

Miles and Directions

0.0   Begin from the trailhead across the paved driveway from the kiosk at the east end of the parking area.

360 feet Stay left at the first two junctions.

0.3   Cross the meadow and reach Meadow Cove Creek.

0.5   Turn left onto the Yellow Trail.

0.6   Turn left onto the ATV Trail at the splitrail fence.

0.7   Turn right onto the White Trail.

1.0   Arrive back at the first junction. Turn left to return to the trailhead.

1.1   Arrive back at the trailhead.

3 Linekin Preserve

The White Trail in Linekin Preserve passes through a mature forest with a carpet of spring wildflowers and ferns, passing an active vernal pool. The trail then reaches the Damariscotta River atop a high bluff with fine views. Before turning back inland, there are two places with easy shore access. On the return, the blue-blazed Burley Loop follows a small stream to overlooks of a swamp and a beaver flowage.

Start: From the trailhead at the east end of the parking area next to the kiosk
Distance: 2.9-mile lollipop
Hiking time: About 2 hours
Difficulty: Easy
Best season: May–Oct
Trail surface: Woodland path and exposed bedrock
Land status: Linekin Preserve
Nearest town: Boothbay Harbor
Other trail users: None

Water availability: None
Canine compatibility: Dogs must be on a leash at all times
Fees and permits: No fees or permits are required
Maps: *DeLorme's The Maine Atlas and Gazetteer map 7; USGS Pemaquid Point*
Trail contact: Boothbay Region Land Trust, (207) 633-4818, www.bbrlt.org

Finding the trailhead: From downtown Camden, drive south 39.7 miles on US 1. Turn left onto ME 27. Drive 10.8 miles to Boothbay Harbor. Turn left onto ME 96 at the traffic light. Drive 3.8 miles, the parking area is on the left. The trail begins at the back of the parking area next to the kiosk. Trailhead GPS: N43 52.711' / W69 40.909'

The Hike

The White Trail descends gently through a mature mixed forest carpeted with spring wildflowers and ferns. In several low spots swamp plants abound. Just before reaching the Damariscotta River, there is an active vernal pool on the right. Look for tadpoles and efts—or if it is before mid-June, egg bundles floating on or in the water.

Across a gravel drive, the trail emerges from the forest atop a high bluff overlooking the Damariscotta River. From here you have an almost unobstructed view of the open, rolling waters of the Gulf of Maine. In the distance, Monhegan Island seems to ride the swell like an ocean liner.

There are two side trail with access to the rocky shore and views up and down the Damariscotta River and Rutherford Island across the narrow channel of the river. Watch for osprey and eagles. In late spring it is not uncommon to see osprey carrying nesting material or eagles in their paired mating flight.

On the return leg of the hike, you can stay on the White Trail or take the Burley Loop. This blue-blazed trail follows a small stream through a forest that may never have been logged. The forest is cool and mossy in deep shade.

The trail comes to an overlook of Little River, a narrow creek that snakes through a marshy swale. Just downstream, out of sight, the stream opens into a small bay. The trail turns north and follows the stream to a second overlook above a beaver flowage. The small impoundment blends into the woods, barely an opening in the forest canopy.

Miles and Directions

0.0   Begin from the trailhead at the east end of the parking area.

0.2   Pass a trail on the right that will be your return trail.

0.6   Pass Yellow Trail on the right.

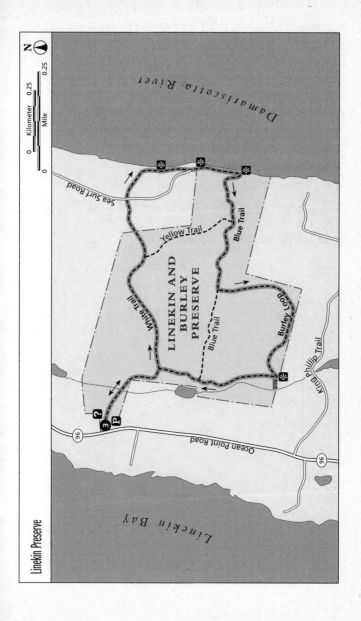

Linekin Preserve

Linekin Bay

Damariscotta River

LINEKIN AND BURLEY PRESERVE

Sea Surf Road

Yellow Trail

White Trail

Blue Trail

Blue Trail

Burley Loop

King Phillip Trail

Ocean Point Road

96

96

P

3

N

0   Kilometer   0.25

0   Mile   0.25

0.8 There is a vernal pool to the right of the trail just before the trail crosses a private lane.

0.9 Reach the Damariscotta River.

1.4 Pass several overlooks and access points to the river. After this last one, the trail turns west away from the river.

1.7 Pass the other end of the Yellow Trail on the right.

1.9 Turn left onto the blue-blazed Burley Loop.

2.4 Follow a small stream to an overlook.

2.6 Overlook of a beaver flowage.

2.7 Arrive back at first junction. Turn left to return to the trailhead.

2.9 Arrive back at the trailhead.

4 Ovens Mouth

The Eastern Shore Loop follows the shore of Cross River—what appears to be a lake surrounded by evergreens but is actually a bay. The trail reaches a rocky point where the river flows out into this bay. The river's narrow channel between rock walls is the Ovens Mouth. The tidal current carries water in or out of the bay at an astonishing speed. A bridge over an inlet connects the Ovens Mouth East and West Trails. The return hike on the Eastern Loop follows along the edge of a marsh at the head of the inlet.

Start: From the Ovens Mouth East trailhead at the end of the dirt road
Distance: 1.6-mile loop
Hiking time: About 2 hours
Difficulty: Easy
Best season: May–Oct
Trail surface: Woodland path
Land status: Ovens Mouth Preserve
Nearest town: Boothbay
Other trail users: None

Water availability: None
Canine compatibility: Dogs must be on a leash at all times
Fees and permits: No fees or permits are required
Maps: *DeLorme's The Maine Atlas and Gazetteer* map 7; *USGS Westport*
Trail contact: Boothbay Region Land Trust, (207) 633-4818, www.bbrlt.org

Finding the trailhead: From downtown Camden, drive south 39.7 miles on US 1. Turn left onto ME 27. Drive 6.1 miles. Turn right onto Adams Pond Road. Drive 0.2 mile. Turn right onto Dover Road. Drive 2.0 miles to the Ovens Mouth East trailhead at the end of the road. The trailhead is at the north end of the parking area next to the kiosk. Trailhead GPS: N43 55.785' / W69 38.380'

The Hike

The Eastern Loop Trail follows the shore of the Cross River, which appears to be a lake with evergreens crowding down to its irregular shoreline. In fact Cross River is a large saltwater cove in the center of Boothbay Peninsula. It is connected to the Sheepscot River by a narrow channel that runs west from the cove. All along the Mid-Coast, bays and rivers—even ponds and creeks—almost all run north-south. It is a function of the sedimentary bedrock. The Cross River cuts across, having found some weakness or fissure in the bedrock.

At a rocky point the cove narrows to a straight channel that flows west between rock walls to the Sheepscot River. This channel is the Ovens Mouth. On an incoming tide the water rushes into the cove at more than 20 miles per hour. Whirlpools and lines of foam race past you as you stand on the shore. Several hours later, the water rushes back out with equal force.

Behind you tower mature white pines. In the top of one the trail passes beneath an osprey nest, a roundish collection of sticks perched on the flattened treetop. The adults seem uncomfortable landing on the nest when hikers are so close, so don't linger too long.

At a narrow inlet that looks more like a creek, the trail turns south, away from the rushing Cross River. A bridge spans the inlet, connecting the East Side Trail with the West Side Trail. For another look at the river, cross the bridge and follow the trail north to a rocky point.

From the bridge, the East Side Trail follows south along the edge of the inlet as it fades into a marsh. On the other side of the marsh, you can see—atop a high bluff—the West

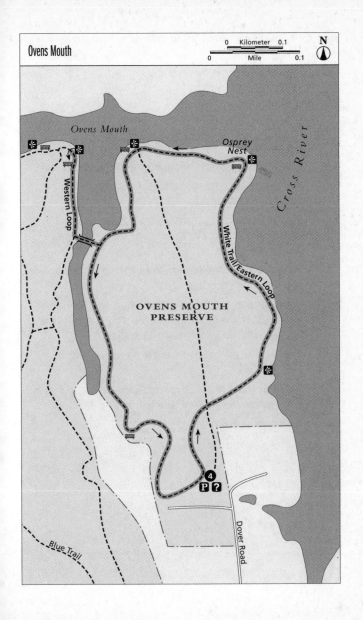

Ovens Mouth

Kilometer
0   0.1
Mile
0   0.1

N

Ovens Mouth

Osprey Nest

Cross River

Western Loop

White Trail/Eastern Loop

OVENS MOUTH
PRESERVE

4
P ?

Blue Trail

Dover Road

Side Trail. Just before the trail turns east toward the trailhead, there is a bench. You can sit and watch for the osprey coming and going or smaller, less showy, birds.

Miles and Directions

0.0   Begin from the East Side Trail trailhead at the north end of the parking area.

0.3   Arrive at the Cross River, which is actually a cove.

0.5   Arrive at a rocky point, where Cross River empties into the cove from Ovens Mouth.

0.7   The trail follows along Ovens Mouth, passing beneath a white pine with an osprey's nest in the crown. Reach a narrow inlet on the left.

0.8   The trail follows the inlet south to a bridge that spans it. Turn right and cross the bridge.

1.0   Across the bridge, turn right onto the West Side Trail and follow it to a rocky point on Ovens Mouth. To complete the hike return the way you came to the bridge.

1.2   Arrive back at the bridge. Cross it and turn right onto the East Side Trail.

1.3   Pass a viewpoint of a boggy stream with a bluff on the other side. You can see the West Side Trail atop the bluff.

1.6   Arrive back at the trailhead.

5 Dodge Point

The hike around Dodge Point Public Reserved Land passes through a mature oak-pine forest along the Ravine Trail through land covered by deep glacial till. The hike passes man-made Ice Pond, which has become a picturesque part of the landscape. Much of the hike is along the shore of the tidal Damariscotta River. The complex geology of the Mid-Coast is on display in the bedrock and beach types. The hike offers shore access to several places that are popular for swimming.

Start: Dodge Point trailhead at the south end of the parking area, to the right of the Information sign

Distance: 3.8-mile loop

Hiking time: About 2 to 3 hours

Difficulty: Moderate

Best season: May–Oct

Trail surface: Woodland path and woods road

Land status: Dodge Point Public Reserved Land

Nearest town: Newcastle

Other trail users: Hunting is permitted in Public Reserved Lands

Water availability: Ice Pond at mile 1.0

Canine compatibility: Dogs need to be under control at all times

Fees and permits: No fees or permits are required

Maps: DeLorme's The Maine Atlas and Gazetteer map 7; USGS Boothbay

Trail contact: Dodge Point Public Reserved Land, (207) 778-8231, www.maine.gov/dacf/parks

Finding the trailhead: From downtown Camden drive 33.5 miles to the junction with ME 215. Take US 1 Business and ME 215 for 0.4 mile into Newcastle. At the Stop sign in Newcastle, stay straight on ME 215. Drive 0.1 mile and turn left onto River Road. Drive 3.2 miles. The parking area is on the left at the black Dodge Point Public Reserved Land sign. Two trails (with the same name) leave from the south end of the parking area. The trailhead is the trail to the right of the Information sign. Trailhead GPS: N43 59.696' / W69 34.059'

The Hike

Dodge Point Public Reserved Land lies near the head of a peninsula between the Sheepscot and Damariscotta Rivers. An old farm road, maintained as a hiking trail, circles around the reserved land; the hiking trails all cross and connect with the road, allowing you to make a loop hike through all of the reserved land east of River Road.

The Ravine Trail winds along the top of a deep ravine that is very atypical of Maine. Almost nowhere in the ravine is there exposed bedrock or even boulders. This part of the Maine coast was covered with ice during the last ice age, but was little changed by the ice sheet. The largest effect was a deep layer of glacial till deposited on the bedrock. The forest floor is blanketed with wildflowers before the trees leaf out and leave everything in deep shade.

Near where the stream drains into the Damariscotta River, a dam was built to create a pond so that its ice could be cut off each winter. Commercial icing was a huge business in the Mid-Coast region from the Civil War until refrigerators became common. The region had abundant freshwater ice and easy access to ships to deliver the ice to markets like New York and Boston. Given the small size of Ice Pond, it is unlikely that its ice ended up in someone's icebox in New York City, but the pond is a reminder of just how much our world has changed in a relatively short time.

The hike crosses the Old Farm Road and follows the Shore Trail out to the Damariscotta River. The woods are no longer an oak-pine forest, but one of almost exclusively evergreens. As you step out onto the shore of the river, you may think that it looks less like a river and more like a narrow bay. In fact, the Damariscotta River is tidal salt water. Most of the boats that use the river are pleasure crafts; you hear very little of the deep, diesel thrum of working boats.

The Shore Trail follows the river in the woods atop a low bluff. Each side trail to the shore leads to a unique beach across different bedrock. In some places the beach is almost sand, in others it is large cobbles or mud flats. Some of the rock shows ripples and swirls like sand in a shallow pool; some of the rock is granite or shale. This complex geology is a function of how the bays and peninsulas of the Mid-Coast were created. The differences in the beaches resulted from how the tide and currents sorted the rocks of different sizes and weights onto the shore.

As you hike, you may pass small groups of people swimming or lounging on the shore. At the southern end of Dodge Point, there is a boat dock built out over a large sheet of bedrock that juts out into the river. Swimmers tend to congregate here.

The hike turns inland and winds back toward the trailhead. Along the Timber Trail, you pass the beginning of the River Link Trail. This trail is part of an effort to create a protected corridor from Newcastle to Boothbay that passes through Dodge Point Public Reserved Land and several land trust preserves, ending at Boothbay Region Land Trust's Zak Preserve. The trail runs down the center of the peninsula, not near or along either shore.

Miles and Directions

0.0   Start from Old Farm Road to the right of the information sign.

300 feet Turn left onto the Ravine Trail.

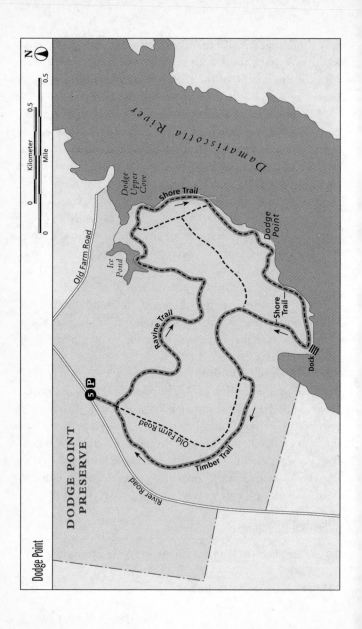

Dodge Point

DODGE POINT PRESERVE

Damariscotta River

Dodge Upper Cove

Dodge Point

Shore Trail

Shore Trail

Ice Pond

Old Farm Road

Ravine Trail

Old Farm Road

Timber Trail

River Road

Dock

N

Kilometer

Mile

0   0.5

0   0.5

0.6	Turn left at an unmarked fork.
1.0	The trail follows the south shore of Ice Pond.
1.2	The Ravine Trail passes around Ice Pond and ends at Old Farm Road. Turn right onto Old Farm Road. After 250 feet, turn left onto the Shore Trail.
1.3	The trail reaches the shore of the Damariscotta River.
1.5	The trail follows the river atop a low bluff with occasional access to the water. The trail comes to an unmarked junction. The trail to the right connects to Old Farm Road. Turn left and you can walk out to the sand beach. The Shore Trail continues along the river in the woods.
1.8	The trail passes around Dodge Point.
1.9	Shore access on interesting bedrock.
2.0	Pass a junction in the woods. It is another trail that leads away from the river to Old Farm Road.
2.3	The trail becomes a woods road. Two hundred feet to your left is a boat dock. Turn right and hike toward Old Farm Road.
2.6	The Shore Trail ends at Old Farm Road. Turn left.
2.9	Turn left onto the Timber Trail.
3.5	The Timber Trail passes the River Link Trail.
3.7	The Timber Trail ends at Old Farm Road. Turn left to return to the trailhead.
3.8	Arrive back at the trailhead.

6 Stetser Preserve

The Blue Trail is a self-guided nature trail that explains the natural history of the preserve. The Red Trail climbs a low hill with several large blueberry patches, then descends to a pond where beaver can be seen. The hike passes through several different forest types with the opportunity to see lots of different wildflowers in season.

Start: From the trailhead at the east end of the parking area, beyond the rocks
Distance: 2.0-mile lollipop
Hiking time: About 1 to 2 hours
Difficulty: Easy
Best season: May–Oct
Trail surface: Woodland path
Land status: Stetser Preserve
Nearest town: Newcastle
Other trail users: Hunting is allowed in season

Water availability: None
Canine compatibility: Dogs need to be on a leash at all times
Fees and permits: No fees or permits are required
Maps: *DeLorme's The Maine Atlas and Gazetteer* map 13; *USGS North Whitefield*
Trail contact: Sheepscot Valley Conservation Association, (207) 586-5616, www.sheepscot.org

Finding the trailhead: From downtown Camden drive south on US 1 for 33.5 miles to the exit for ME 215. Turn right off the exit, driving north on ME 215 for 5.3 miles. Go straight, onto ME 194. Drive 2.3 miles. Turn right onto Egypt Road. Drive 2.6 miles. The Stetser Preserve parking area is on the right. The trailhead is at the east end of the parking area beyond the rocks. Trailhead GPS: N44 08.144' / W69 34.514'

The Hike

The trail crosses a low, wet area that drains into the pond you will pass near the end of the hike. After the fork, the trail climbs gently to an opening in the forest where the bedrock is exposed. The hike crosses several such patches of bedrock. They are covered with dry, brittle lichen and surrounded by blueberries, strongly suggesting this area's bedrock is granite. People tend to think of granite as the stuff of mountains: Katahdin in northern Maine and Cadillac Mountain in Acadia National Park. In fact, much of Maine's granite is under lowlands like the Stetser Preserve.

After the seventh marker on the self-guided nature trail, the hike follows the Red Trail. You miss numbers 8 through 11 on the nature trail, but pass many more blueberries. The Red Trail wanders south, keeping to the same elevation. Past the last of the blueberries, the trail drops into wetter, shady woods. Just a difference of 50 feet of elevation completely changes the forest.

A marked side trail leads down to a pond. Look for beaver, making a distinctive V as their noses push through the water. The side trail ends where the wet area you recently hiked through on the Red Trail drains into the pond.

The trail follows an old woods road for a distance, a reminder that these woods were probably farmland in an earlier time. You pass the Blue Trail and the last few markers on the nature trail before arriving back at the trailhead.

Miles and Directions

0.0   Start from the trailhead beyond the rocks at the east end of the parking area.

0.1   The trail enters the woods and crosses through a low, wet area to a fork. Bear left and climb.

0.3   Junction with the Red Trail. Bear left, leaving the Blue Trail. (**Option:** You can turn right, staying on the Blue Trail and

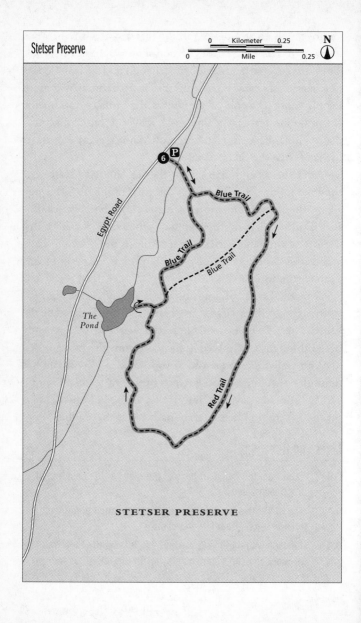

Stetser Preserve

0   Kilometer   0.25

0   Mile   0.25

N

Egypt Road

P
6

Blue Trail

Blue Trail

Blue Trail

The Pond

Red Trail

STETSER PRESERVE

following the self-guided nature trail. This shorter hike is 1.0 mile.)

1.4 The Red Trail loops over a low ridge with many semi-open areas of blueberries, then drops into a wet area arriving at a T intersection. Turn left and descend to the pond.

1.5 The trail ends where a small stream flows into the pond. To continue the hike, return to the T intersection.

1.6 At the T intersection, go straight.

1.7 The Red Trail ends at the Blue Trail. Go straight to return to the trailhead.

1.9 Arrive back at the fork. Turn left to return to the trailhead.

2.0 Arrive back at the trailhead.

7 Crooked Farm

The Crook Trail crosses a meadow, then follows upstream along the Pemaquid River through a ferny woods. After leaving the river, a side trail leads north to Boyd Pond—a wide spot in the river. The hike heads back toward the trailhead over higher ground through a dry mixed forest.

Start: From the trailhead at the northwest corner of the parking area
Distance: 2.5-mile lollipop
Hiking time: About 2 to 3 hours
Difficulty: Easy
Best season: May–Oct
Trail surface: Woodland path
Land status: Crooked Farm Nature Preserve
Nearest town: New Harbor
Other trail users: The preserve is open to hunting in season

Water availability: Pemaquid River
Canine compatibility: Dogs must be on a leash at all times
Fees and permits: No fees or permits are required
Maps: *DeLorme's The Maine Atlas and Gazetteer* map 7; *USGS Bristol*
Trail contact: Pemaquid Watershed Association, (207) 563-2196, www.pemaquidwatershed .org

Finding the trailhead: From downtown Camden drive south on US 1 for 24.0 miles to the light in Waldoboro. Turn left onto ME 32. Drive 16.5 miles. Turn right onto Foster Road. Drive 1.3 miles. Turn right onto ME 130. Drive 0.2 mile. Turn right onto Old County Road. Drive 0.8 mile. The trailhead parking area is on the left. The trailhead is next to the kiosk in the northwest corner of the parking area. Trailhead GPS: N43 54.988' / W69° 30.230'

The Hike

The Crook Trail descends along the edge of a large meadow to a junction with Pine Loop Trail. This short trail leads

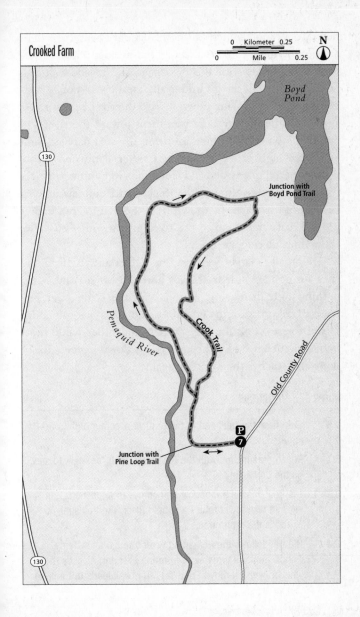

Crooked Farm

0 Kilometer 0.25
0 Mile 0.25

N

Boyd Pond

Junction with Boyd Pond Trail

Pemaquid River

Crook Trail

Old County Road

P 7

Junction with Pine Loop Trail

130

130

down to a canoe launch on the Pemaquid River. Turn right and follow the Crook Trail across the meadow. Several species of butterflies visit the flowers in the meadow during summer. Much of the ground in the meadow is spongy, suggesting water is moving down toward the river beneath you.

Across the meadow the trail turns toward the river and enters the woods. You hike upstream through dappled light and knee-high ferns. Maples and other hardwoods grow widely spaced in a wide band along the river. In many places the river spreads out into alder thickets, the trail staying well back from the water. In a few places the trail follows higher ground that fingers out to the river, giving you good views of the meandering stream.

Eventually a larger wet area forces the trail away from the river for good. A side trial leads north to Boyd Pond, really nothing more than a long sinuous widening of the river. The Crook Trail turns south and climbs enough to get into a dry mixed forest. Look for lady slippers and other wildflowers found in such woods. The trail drops down a steep, rocky slope and reaches the meadow again.

Miles and Directions

0.0   Start from the trailhead at the northwest corner of the parking area.

0.1   Reach the junction with the Pine Loop Trail. Turn right to stay on the Crook Trail.

0.3   The trail crosses a meadow and comes to a junction. Turn left and hike toward the Pemaquid River. The trail straight ahead is the return trail.

1.4   The trail follows the Pemaquid River through a low ferny woods. The trail turns away from the river and reaches the junction with the Boyd Pond Trail. This trail leads 0.3 mile to the shore of Boyd Pond. Turn right to continue on the Crook Trail.

2.2 The trail passes through a dry conifer forest, then drops down to a junction. Go straight to return to the trailhead.

2.5 Arrive back at the trailhead.

8 LaVerna Preserve

The Hoyt Trail drops through open woods, carpeted with ferns and spring wildflowers, to the marshy Meadow Brook. The Ellis Trail passes through an oak–pine forest to the shore with an unobstructed view of the open sea. The shore is steep, irregular bedrock all the way around Browns Head Cove to Leighton Head. A side trail leads out onto the bedrock, thin upturned layers of slate. The Tibbitts Trail follows farther south along the coast among spruce. Look for the osprey nest near the trail. After one last side trail out onto the rock, the trail turns inland and climbs away from the shore.

Start: From the Hoyt Trail trailhead across ME 32 from the parking area
Distance: 3.4-mile lollipop
Hiking time: About 2 to 3 hours
Difficulty: Moderate
Best season: May–Oct
Trail surface: Woodland path
Land status: LaVerna Preserve
Nearest town: Round Pond
Other trail users: None

Water availability: None
Canine compatibility: Dogs must be on a leash at all times
Fees and permits: None
Maps: *DeLorme's The Maine Atlas and Gazetteer* map 7; USGS Louds Island
Trail contact: Pemaquid Watershed Association, (207) 563-2196, www.pemaquidwatershed.org

---

Finding the trailhead: From downtown Camden drive south on US 1 for 24.0 miles to the light in Waldoboro. Turn left onto ME 32. Drive 16.9 miles. The trailhead parking area is on the right side of the road. The trailhead is across ME 32 from the parking area. Trailhead GPS: N43 54.164' / W69 28.786'

The Hike

The Hoyt Trail winds through a hardwood forest to Meadow Brook. The narrow, gravel-bottomed stream with lily pads floating on the surface winds from a marsh upstream southward to the sea. Across the bridge the forest changes to one dominated by evergreens.

The Ellis Trail loops north through this dry oak-pine forest to the shore. The trail reaches the steep, rocky shore near Browns Head. A side trail leads out onto the rocks above the surf. In front of you is an unobstructed view of the Atlantic Ocean. In the distance you can see Monhegan Island.

The trail continues south along the rounded arc of the cove to Leighton Head. The LaVerna Trail leads out onto the exposed bedrock. You can climb onto and over upturned layers of dark shale shot through with dykes of harder, newer rock. It is the rugged coastline on the Mid-Coast.

The Tibbitts Trail continues south along the shore through a spruce forest with many storm-killed trees over zoophylic ground. The difference in the forest south of Leighton Head suggests that the bedrock here is different, probably granite. All along the Mid-Coast there are narrow bands of granite that were injected into the shale bedrock as it was deformed by tectonic movement 400 million years ago. Look for the osprey nest balanced atop one of the taller trees.

Beyond a marked side trail that leads out onto the rocks, high above the water, the trail turns inland and climbs away from the shore. You get a view straight out to the osprey nest. If you are hiking in June or early July, you may see chicks in the nest.

The Tibbitts Trail heads inland though wet forest where cedars lean this way and that before ending at the LaVerna

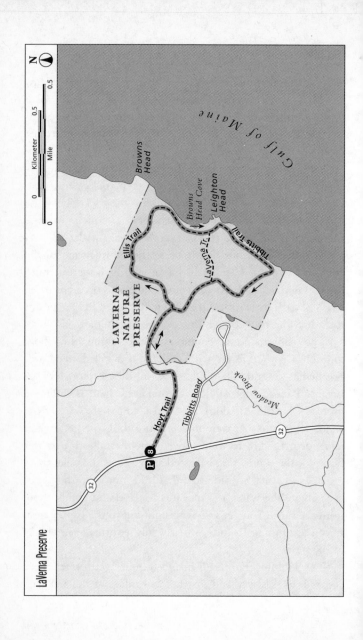

Laverna Preserve

N

Gulf of Maine

Browns Head

Browns Head Cove

Leighton Head

Ellis Trail

Laverna Tr.

Tibbits Trail

LAVERNA
NATURE
PRESERVE

Hoyt Trail

Tibbits Road

Meadow Brook

32

P 8

32

Kilometer

Mile

0   0.5

0   0.5

Trail. You'll be tempted to turn right and head back out to Leighton Head rather than turning left and heading back to your car.

Miles and Directions

0.0   Start from the Hoyt Trailhead across ME 32 from the parking area.

0.5   The trail changes name to the LaVerna Trail when you enter the LaVerna Preserve.

0.7   Turn left onto the yellow-blazed Ellis Trail.

1.4   The trail reaches the coast near Browns Head.

1.7   The Ellis Trail ends at the LaVerna Trail. Turn left onto the LaVerna Trail toward the shore.

1.8   Reach the end of the LaVerna Trail. A short side trail leads out onto Leighton Head. The hike continues on the Tibbitts Trail south along the shore.

2.1   A short side trail leads out onto the rocky shore. The Tibbitts Trail turns right and climbs away from the coast.

2.5   Arrive back at the LaVerna Trail. Turn left to hike back to the trailhead.

2.7   Pass the Ellis Trail. Bear left to return to the trailhead.

3.4   Arrive back at the trailhead.

9 Hockomock Nature Trail

The trail winds through a mixed forest dominated by white pine to Hockomock Point, with several self-guided nature trail markers along the way. Across a narrow channel is Hog Island, the Audubon camp buildings visible along the shore. To the west is Muscongus Sound. The trail goes east along Keene Narrows, past the boat dock. The Pine Trail continues along the shore, then loops back through piney woods to the trailhead.

Start: From the trailhead on the right side of the road 100 feet down the hill from the visitor center

Distance: 1.2-mile loop

Hiking time: About 1 to 2 hours

Difficulty: Easy

Best season: May–Oct

Trail surface: Woodland path

Land status: Todd Wildlife Sanctuary

Nearest town: Waldoboro

Other trail users: None

Water availability: None

Canine compatibility: Dogs are not permitted in the Todd Wildlife Sanctuary

Fees and permits: None

Maps: *DeLorme's The Maine Atlas and Gazetteer* map 7; *USGS Louds Island*

Trail contact: Todd Wildlife Sanctuary, (207) 529-5148, www.hogisland.audubon.org/todd-wildlife-sanctuary

Finding the trailhead: From downtown Camden drive 24.0 miles south on US 1 to the light in Waldoboro. Turn left onto ME 32. Drive 7.6 miles. Turn left onto Keene Neck Road at the Audubon sign. Drive 1.5 miles to the Todd Wildlife Sanctuary. Turn left into the sanctuary. The visitor center and trailhead are straight ahead on the right. Trailhead GPS: N43 59.038' / W69 25.179'

The Hike

The Todd Wildlife Sanctuary is the jumping-off point for Hog Island, home of the Audubon Society's adult and family summer camps. From the visitor center, you can look down across a grassy meadow to the boat dock. A hundred feet offshore is darkly wooded Hog Island. Near the north end of the island you can see white buildings that house the camp. Beyond Hog Island is the island-choked Medomak River, which separates Keene Neck from the town of Friendship.

You can admire this view as you hike across the meadow toward the dark forest on the Hockomock Nature Trail. This self-guided nature trail passes ancient field oaks that are now surrounded by forest, wildlife, and mica-specked granite bedrock, all explained in the brochure available at the trailhead.

At Hockomock Point you can go out onto the rocks and wander among the boulders at low tide. Hog Island is close enough you might be able to throw a rock to it. The trail follows along the narrow channel, then emerges from the forest and back into the meadow. Watch for broken pieces of white shells mixed into the trail. You are walking over a shell midden, a place where Indians tossed their harvested shells as long as 3,000 years ago.

Stay close to the shore past the boat dock and begin to walk up the gravel road. Turn onto the Pine Tree Trail (or continue up the road past the pond to the trailhead). The Pine Tree Trail reenters the woods—here almost entirely white pine—and heads north along Keene Narrows between the shore and Oar Island. The trail wanders through the woods, ending across the gravel road from the trailhead.

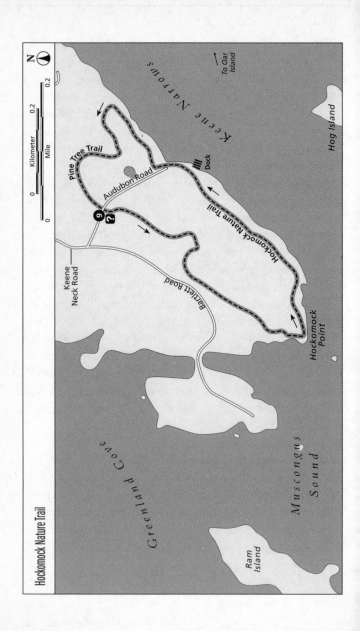

Hockomock Nature Trail

Miles and Directions

0.0   Start from the Hockomock Nature Trail trailhead 100 feet down the gravel road from the visitor center.

0.5   The trail crosses a meadow, enters the woods, and reaches the shore at Hockomock Point.

0.8   The trail follows the shoreline to the end of the gravel road near the dock and boathouse. Follow the blazes around the shore side of the dock house and continue up the road.

0.9   Turn right, leaving the road, onto the Pine Tree Trail. The trail enters the woods and follows the shoreline north.

1.0   The trail turns inland away from the shore.

1.2   Arrive back at the trailhead.

10 Martin Point

The trail through the Martin Point Preserve first passes Crystal Pond—a picture-perfect freshwater pond surrounded by forest within sight of the ocean. A short walk along its shore leads to a beaver lodge. The trail crosses Martin Point, heading west through a carpet of pine needles beneath mature pines. The trail drops down to within sight of Muscongus Bay before climbing past the granite outcropping known as Judy's Ledges. The hike follows an abandoned woods road back to the trailhead.

Start: From the trailhead at the north end of the parking area beyond the kiosk

Distance: 1.6-mile loop

Hiking time: About 1 to 2 hours

Difficulty: Easy

Best season: May–Oct

Trail surface: Woodland path

Land status: Martin Point Wildlife Reserve

Nearest town: Friendship

Other trail users: None

Water availability: None

Canine compatibility: Dogs must be on a leash at all times

Fees and permits: None

Maps: *DeLorme's The Maine Atlas and Gazetteer* map 7; *USGS Friendship*

Trail contact: Medomak Valley Land Trust, (207) 832-5570, www.medomakvalley.org

Finding the trailhead: From downtown Camden drive 15.5 miles south on US 1 to ME 97. Turn left onto ME 97. Drive 9.6 miles into Friendship. Turn right onto ME 220. Drive 0.4 mile. Turn left onto Martin Point Road. Drive 2.4 miles. The trailhead parking area is on the right. The trailhead is at the north end of the parking area. Trailhead GPS: N43 58.147' / W69 22.024'

The Hike

Martin Point Road hugs the western shore of Hatchet Cove. Lobster boats rock on their moorings offshore of the working dock, piled high with lobster pots. It is a scene you would expect to find Downeast, not amid the second homes and tourist shops of the Mid-Coast. Watch for a turnout just before the road turns west to cross Martin Point. There is a beach where you can swim, wade, or just contemplate the view.

The hike begins in a second-growth forest with large open patches where an abandoned logging road ran down the spine of Martin Point. As you hike toward Crystal Pond, watch for wildflowers, including lady slipper orchids.

Crystal Pond is a small freshwater pond within sight of Hatchet Cove. The south end of the pond, where you first see it, is a marsh that spills over into the woods, leaving naked snags standing in the shallow water amid an explosion of sedges, water lilies, and water hyacinth. An unmarked trail follows north along the shore of the pond to two beaver lodges. The lodges are right near the shore, together, as if the beavers outgrew the first lodge and added on. If you are quiet, especially at dawn or dusk, you may see a beaver making a V through the water with a branch in its mouth.

From the pond the trail climbs onto the spine of the point and into a mature pine forest. Across the abandoned logging road, the trail drops down through spruce to Muscongus Bay. Someone has hung dozens of lobster buoys in the trees along the trail. Just before it reaches the water, the trail turns back inland and climbs, the trees decorated for a lobsterman's holiday. The trail winds through a group of boulders and climbs a low rock face called Judy's Ledges.

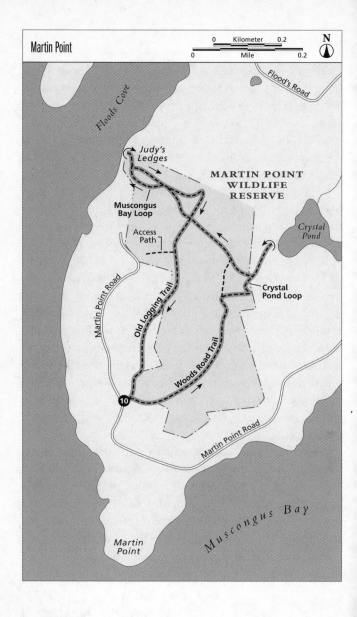

Martin Point

Kilometer 0.2
Mile 0.2

N

Flood's Road

Floods Cove

Judy's
Ledges

MARTIN POINT
WILDLIFE
RESERVE

Muscongus
Bay Loop

Crystal
Pond

Access
Path

Old Logging Trail

Crystal
Pond Loop

Woods Road Trail

Martin Point Road

10

Martin Point Road

Muscongus Bay

Martin
Point

Once back on the spine of the point, the hike follows the abandoned logging road back to the trailhead. The road is paved, most of the way, with rusty pine needles that have accumulated over the years, adding a hush to the walk.

Miles and Directions

0.0   Follow the blue-blazed Woods Road Trail, which goes to the right (east) from the trailhead. The gold-blazed Old Logging Trail is the return trail.

0.3   Turn right onto the yellow-blazed Crystal Pond Loop.

0.5   The trail comes to a beaver lodge near the shore of the pond.

0.6   Continue straight, following the red blazes. The map here (and elsewhere in the reserve) is not correct.

0.7   Arrive back at the Woods Road Trail. Turn right.

0.8   Cross the Old Logging Trail onto the green-blazed Muscongus Bay Trail.

0.9   Reach the low bluff along the shore. There is no access to the shore and only limited views through the thick spruce. Turn right and climb away from the shore.

1.0   The trail passes beneath and then climbs Judy's Ledges.

1.2   The Muscongus Bay Trail ends at the gold-blazed Old Logging Trail. Turn right to head back to the trailhead.

1.6   Arrive back at the trailhead.

11 Nelson Nature Preserve

The hike follows South Trail through evergreens along the most picturesque stone wall. The trail then drops down into a maple swamp with an understory of skunk cabbage. The trail continues all the way to the Goose River, but unfortunately is too wet to follow beyond the Swamp Trail. This trail cuts across to Middle Trail—it is often very wet as its name suggests. Middle Trail climbs back toward the trailhead through a mostly dry mixed forest with a variety of wildflowers in the understory.

Start: From the trailhead at the west end of the parking area next to the kiosk

Distance: 1.3-mile lollipop

Hiking time: About 1 to 2 hours

Difficulty: Easy

Best season: May–Oct

Trail surface: Woodland path and wet bog

Land status: Nelson Nature Preserve

Nearest town: Friendship (no services) and Waldoboro

Other trail users: None

Water availability: None

Canine compatibility: Dog are not allowed in the preserve

Fees and permits: None

Maps: *DeLorme's The Maine Atlas and Gazetteer* map 7; *USGS Friendship* and *Waldoboro East*

Trail contact: Maine Audubon, (207) 781-2330, maine audubon.org

Finding the trailhead: From downtown Camden drive 15.5 miles south on US 1 to ME 97. Turn left onto ME 97. Drive 8.2 miles. The preserve is on the left. There is a hard-to-see wooden sign just before the drive up into the parking area. The preserve entrance is 1.4 miles from the junction of ME 97 and ME 220 in Friendship. The trailhead is at the west end of the parking area next to the information kiosk. Trailhead GPS: N43 59.951' / W69 19.122'

The Hike

The South Trail follows a moss-covered stone wall north into the Nelson Nature Preserve. The wall runs straight, built before the forest was here. Now it blends into the forest like a tree or boulder. The trail moves up and down like a roller coaster over small rocky rises through a dry pine forest. Look for lady slipper orchids and other wildflowers that thrive in acidic soil.

Beyond the Bluff Trail, the trail drops down toward a red maple swamp, a rare forest type in this part of Maine. Swamp maples are among the first trees to change color in the fall, turning scarlet as early as early September. Because of its proximity to the coast, this forest is popular with migrating warblers.

South Trail passes Swamp Trail and disappears into a tangle of maple trees, skunk cabbage, bushes, and water. The trail continues another half mile to Goose River. If you don't mind slogging through water the entire way—or brought knee-high boots—it is a beautiful and unique hike. For the rest of us, the best bet is to cut across on the Swamp Trail to the Middle Trail. The Swamp Trail has several wet sections, but can generally be navigated without getting too wet. It gives you a small taste of the red maple swamp between it and Goose River.

The Middle Trail, too, goes all the way to Goose River, but it is impassibly wet. Turn right and climb away from the swamp into the dry piney forest. Cut across the East Trail to get back to the South Trail through a swale. The trail winds among open water and skunk cabbage, a pocket version of the red maple swamp.

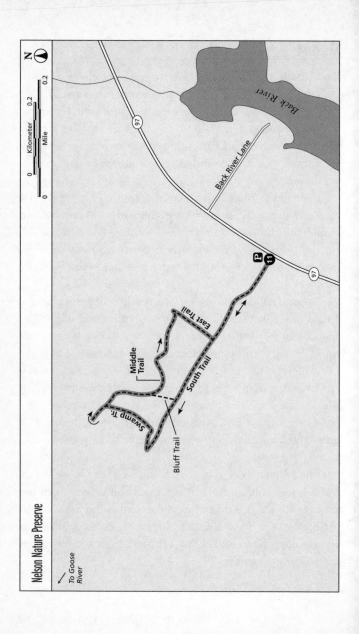

Nelson Nature Preserve

To Goose
River

N

Kilometer
0   0.2

Mile
0   0.2

97

96

Back River Lane

Back River

Middle
Trail

East Trail

South Trail

Bluff Trail

Swamp Tr.

Miles and Directions

0.0   Start on the South Trail at the west end of the parking area next to the sign.

0.2   Pass the East Trail. Continue straight on the South Trail along the stone wall.

0.3   Pass the Bluff Trail.

0.4   Turn right onto the Swamp Trail. The South Trail continues straight ahead, but is too wet for walking without knee-high, waterproof boots.

0.6   Turn right onto the Middle Trail. The Middle Trail to the left goes all the way to Goose River, but like the South Trail is too wet for easy hiking.

0.8   Cross the Bluff Trail.

1.0   Turn right onto the East Trail.

1.1   Arrive back at the South Trail. Turn left to return to the trailhead.

1.3   Arrive back at the trailhead.

12 Pleasant Mountain

The hike follows the Georges Highland Path through a gated pasture with grazing steers and into the woods. You climb gently on an abandoned road, then more steeply on a footpath. The trail passes an ancient field maple just before breaking out of the woods into a blueberry meadow. The trail climbs through the meadow with fine views, only the view east is blocked by Pleasant Mountain. The Georges Highland Path continues east, slabbing around the mountain without climbing it.

Start: From the trailhead at the south end of the parking area next to the kiosk
Distance: 2.4-mile out-and-back
Hiking time: About 2 to 3 hours
Difficulty: Moderate
Best season: May–Oct; late July–Aug for blueberries
Trail surface: Woodland path
Land status: Georges Highland Path on private property
Nearest town: South Hope
Other trail users: Hunting is permitted in season

Water availability: None
Canine compatibility: The trail passes through a working farm with animals; dogs are not encouraged
Fees and permits: None
Maps: *DeLorme's The Maine Atlas and Gazetteer* map 14; *USGS West Rockport*
Trail Contact: Georges River Land Trust, (207) 594-5166, www.georgesriver.org

Finding the trailhead: From downtown Camden, drive 1.8 miles south on US 1 to ME 90. Turn right and drive 2.7 miles to ME 17. Turn right and drive 4.0 miles into South Hope. Turn left onto Harts Mill Road. Drive 0.2 mile. Turn left onto Fogler Road. Drive 1.2 miles. When Fogler Road makes a sharp right, go straight onto a roughly paved road. Almost immediately turn left onto a grassy lane that is the parking area for the hike. There is a sign at the lane. The trailhead is just beyond the kiosk at the south end of the parking area. Trailhead GPS: N44 11.656' / W69 11.588'

The Hike

The Georges Highland Path follows a farm's lane past the barn and house to a pasture gate. Through the gate you cross a meadow watched by grazing steers. Look for the killdeer that nest on the ground in the pasture. Across the pasture the trail passes through a second gate and enters the woods on an old road. The path feels more like a rocky creek than anything else as you walk beneath tall hardwoods.

The trail leaves the old road bed, heading east up the shoulder of Pleasant Mountain, passing an ancient, gnarled field maple. This tree, barely alive, began its life in a pasture. You can tell by the spreading branches—notice the trees around it grow straight for 40 feet or more before there are any branches.

The trail emerges from the woods and crosses a blueberry field. Small oaks and other trees have begun encroaching into the meadow. In another 50 years, these blueberries will be only a memory, like the pasture that maple grew up in. As you climb through the meadow, views open up in every direction but east. The tree-covered mound of Pleasant Mountain blocks that view. Rolling forest broken by occasional farmland and ponds stretches on to the horizon. To the north, on a clear day, you can see Frye and Hogback Mountains.

The Georges Highland Path reenters the woods and continues east to ME 17 across the highway from the trailhead for Ragged Mountain. The trail slabs around the northern flanks of Pleasant and Spruce Mountains without

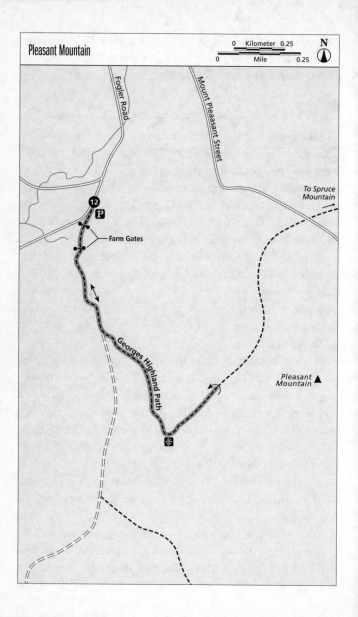

Pleasant Mountain

0   Kilometer   0.25
0   Mile   0.25

N

Fogler Road

Mount Pleasant Street

To Spruce
Mountain

P

Farm Gates

Georges Highland Path

Pleasant
Mountain

climbing either of the wooded summits. To complete your hike you can return directly from the blueberry meadow or hike eastward another 0.2 mile through semi-open hardwood forest to an open slab of bedrock. Beyond this point the trail descends into the valley before crossing Mount Pleasant Street.

Miles and Directions

0.0   Start from the trailhead at the south end of the parking area just beyond the kiosk.

0.1   The trail passes through a line of trees, then continues down the farm lane to a pasture gate. Go through the gate, making sure to close it behind you.

0.2   Cross the pasture to a second gate. Again, make sure to close the gate behind you. The trail turns right after the gate and follows the fence line for 200 feet, then turns left and enters the woods, following an old woods road.

0.4   The trail bears left and leaves the woods road.

0.8   The trail passes an ancient, gnarled field maple.

0.9   The trail leaves the woods and crosses a blueberry field with fine views.

1.0   The trial crosses an ATV trail and reenters the woods.

1.2   The trail skirts around Pleasant Mountain, crossing a semi-open ledge with some views. The Georges Highland Path continues to ME 17, skirting but not climbing Pleasant and Spruce Mountains. To complete the hike, stop here and return the way you came.

2.4   Arrive back at the trailhead.

13 Beech Hill Preserve

This hike climbs gently through a commercial blueberry barren to the summit of Beech Hill. On the summit is a recently renovated lodge surrounded by a lawn with views in every direction. To the north and northeast is a line of mountains: Pleasant, Ragged, and Bald Mountains and Mount Megunticook. Most show bare western faces. To the east you will see a curve of coastline. Islands dot the ocean beyond.

Start: From the Summit Road trailhead at the northwest corner of the parking area next to the kiosk

Distance: 1.2-mile out-and-back

Hiking time: About 1 to 2 hours

Difficulty: Moderate

Best season: May–Oct

Trail surface: Woodland path and lane

Land status: Beech Hill Preserve

Nearest town: Rockport

Other trail users: None

Water availability: None

Canine compatibility: Dogs must be on a leash at all times

Fees and permits: None

Maps: *DeLorme's The Maine Atlas and Gazetteer* map 14; *USGS Camden*

Trail contact: Coastal Mountains Land Trust, (207) 236-7091, www.coastalmountains.org

Finding the trailhead: From downtown Camden, drive south 2.3 miles on US 1. Turn right onto Beech Hill Road. Drive 1.6 miles. The parking area is on the left. Trailhead GPS: N44 10.206' / W69 06.433'

The Hike

The trail heads northeast through woods along Beech Hill Road, then turns southeast and follows a gravel drive up Beech Hill. To your right is a commercial blueberry barren.

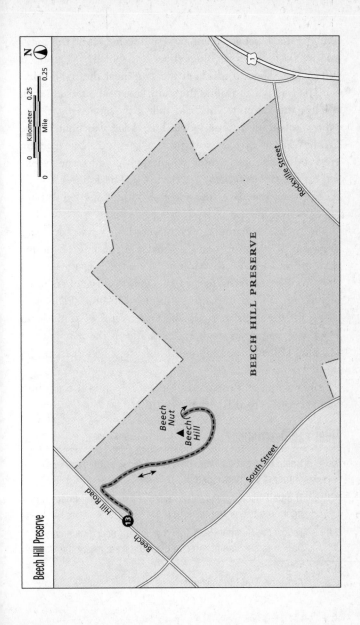

Beech Hill Preserve

The organic blueberries are harvested to help fund the operation of the preserve. Blueberries and blueberry products can be purchased in season at the shop near the trailhead.

The trail winds around the south side of the hill and then reaches the summit. The bald hilltop is capped by Beech Nut, a sod-roofed stone lodge. The lodge was built before World War I as a make-work project, keeping a construction crew busy through winter when they couldn't be working on the owners' home on the coast. The lodge has been recently renovated by the Coastal Mountains Land Trust after years of neglect.

From its wraparound porch, you have views in every direction. To the north and northeast is the line of mountains from Pleasant to Mount Megunticook, most with steep, rocky west faces. To the east a gentle curve of coastline blends into the St. George Peninsula. Offshore, Penobscot Bay is filled with islands: North Haven, Vinal Haven, Isle au Haut, and numerous smaller islands. Across the bay you can see Blue Hill and the mountains of Mount Desert Island on the horizon.

Below you, on the eastern slope of Beech Hill, is another trail accessible from Rockville Road.

Miles and Description

0.0   Begin from the trailhead next to the kiosk at the northeast corner of the parking area.

0.1   The trail follows along Beech Hill Road to Summit Road. Turn right onto this gravel track.

0.6   Follow the Summit Road Trail through a working blueberry barren to the summit. To complete the hike, return the way you came.

1.2   Arrive back at the trailhead.

14 Ragged Mountain

The hike up Ragged Mountain is part of a network of trails from the headwaters of St. George River in Montville to its mouth in Thomaston. The trail up Ragged Mountain, through oak-pine forest, crosses several old stone walls before climbing the mountain's south ridge. From the south ridge, covered with stunted oak trees and blueberries, you have fine views of the surrounding country and Penobscot Bay. The hike ends at the top of the cliffs on Ragged Mountain's west face, which gives it its name. The summit of the mountain is on the spruce-covered ridge to the north.

Start: From the Georges Highland Path trailhead at the north end of the parking area
Distance: 4.8-mile out-and-back
Hiking time: 3 to 4 hours
Difficulty: More challenging
Best season: May–Oct
Trail surface: Woodland path
Land status: Georges River Land Trust preserve
Nearest town: Rockport

Other trail users: None
Water availability: None
Canine compatibility: Dogs must be under control at all times
Fees and permits: None
Maps: *Delorme:* The Maine Atlas and Gazetteer: map 14; USGS *West Rockport*
Trail contact: Georges River Land Trust, (207) 594-5166, www.georgesriver.org

Finding the trailhead: From the junction of US 1 and ME 90 in Rockport, take ME 90 and drive 2.8 miles to the junction of ME 90 and ME 17. Turn right onto ME 17. Drive 1.8 miles to the Georges Highland Path trailhead parking area on the right at the sign. The trailhead is at the north end of the parking area. Trailhead GPS: N44 12.125' / W69 09.543'

The Hike

The trail up Ragged Mountain is part of the larger Georges Highland Path. The Georges Highland Path is not one continuous trail, but a series of short trails from the headwaters of the St. George River in Montville to the mouth of the river in Thomaston. There are 45 miles of trails in this network, with more in the works. The longest stretch of trail is over Ragged Mountain. From the trailhead you can also hike west up Spruce Mountain with fine views of Ragged Mountain and Penobscot Bay. Across Ragged Mountain to the east is the trail up Bald Mountain, with its bare, rocky ledges.

In between, the hike up Ragged Mountain begins in an oak-pine forest that was once a farm. Stone walls cross the trail in several places. The last wall incorporates a natural rock ledge that the trail climbs. The trail crosses a small stream, then turns south along the jumbled rocks at the base of Ragged Mountain's nearly vertical west face. As the trail approaches Mirror Lake, it turns east and climbs steeply. Once up on the ridge, the trail switchbacks and comes to an open ledge with the first views of the hike.

The trail continues to climb with views through oak trees that are stunted and twisted in Dr. Seuss shapes. This open, rocky forest allows enough light to reach the ground for blueberries to thrive, especially along the several ledges the trail crosses. At just over 1,000 feet of elevation, you get your first open view of the Camden Hills and Penobscot Bay to the east. The trail then ducks back into the trees and climbs to the top of the cliffs.

Atop the cliffs you have fine views in every direction. There is a tower on the highest point. This is not Ragged

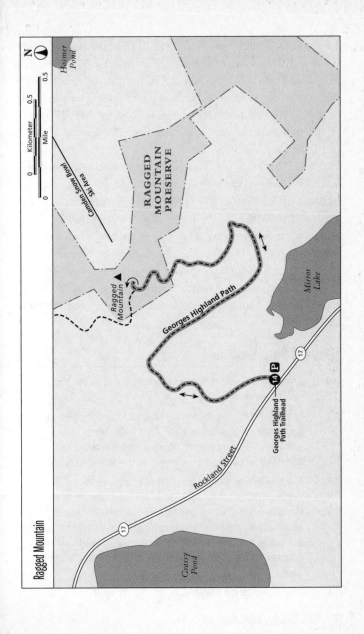

Ragged Mountain

Hosmer Pond

Camden Snow Bowl Ski Area

N

Kilometer
0   0.5
Mile
0   0.5

RAGGED
MOUNTAIN
PRESERVE

Ragged
Mountain

Georges Highland Path

Mirror
Lake

14 P

17

Georges Highland
Path Trailhead

Rockland Street

17

Grassy
Pond

Mountain's summit, but is the end of the hike. The summit is on the spruce-covered ridge to the north. The Georges Highland Path continues across the summit and descends to the north. A mile from the cliffs, the trail forks: The west fork drops down to Gilette Road, a side road off ME 17 north of the trailhead; the east fork descends to Barnestown Road north of Camden Snow Bowl.

From the cliffs on Ragged Mountain, you cannot see Camden Snow Bowl, the town-owned ski area on the mountain's east face. There is a rough trail that begins around the east side of the tower and descends the ski slopes of Camden Snow Bowl. This trail is part of a network of mountain biking trails on the mountain. The best views on the mountain, though, are those from the hike up Ragged Mountain's west side. Camden Snow Bowl is the only ski resort in the United States within view of the Atlantic Ocean.

Miles and Directions

0.0   Start at the Georges Highland Path trailhead at the north end of the parking area.

1.7   The trail heads straight toward Ragged Mountain, then turns south and skirts along its flank. As it nears Mirror Lake, the trail turns east and climbs. Above a switchback the trail comes to an open area with views to the west and south.

2.4   The trail climbs through an open oak forest of stunted trees with intermittent views, arriving at the top of the ridge with views in every direction but east. The summit of Ragged Mountain is along the spruce-covered ridge to the north. An unmarked trail goes around to the east with views in that direction of Bald Mountain and the Camden Hills. To complete the hike, return the way you came.

4.8   Arrive back at the trailhead.

15 Hatchet Mountain

This hike switchbacks up the side of Hatchet Mountain on the road built to get to the cell tower on the summit. The broken rock underfoot and along the trail is stained bright orange with iron. From open areas along the way, you get views of Hobbs Pond at the foot of the mountain and the Camden Hills beyond. Near the summit the view opens up to include Penobscot Bay, seen between Mount Megunticook and Bald Mountain.

Start: From the gate at the west end of the parking area
Distance: 1.6-mile out-and-back
Hiking time: About 2 hours
Difficulty: More challenging
Best season: May–Oct
Trail surface: Gravel road and exposed bedrock
Land status: Hatchet Mountain Preserve
Nearest town: Hope

Other trail users: None
Water availability: None
Canine compatibility: Dogs must be on a leash at all times
Fees and permits: None
Maps: *DeLorme's The Maine Atlas and Gazetteer* map 14: *USGS Searsmont*
Trail contact: Coastal Mountains Land Trust, (207) 236-7091, www.coastalmountains.org

Finding the trailhead: From downtown Camden, drive north for 6.6 miles on ME 105. In the town of Hope, turn left onto ME 235. Drive 0.7 mile. The parking area is on the right. The parking area is small, and ME 235 is sometimes busy. Try to park so you don't have to back out onto the road. Trailhead GPS: N44 15.700' / W69 10.512'

The Hike

The hike climbs Hatchet Mountain on the road built to access the towers on the summit. It is not the most natural or scenic path to follow, but the roadbed is mostly broken shards of sedimentary bedrock stained bright orange by iron. The hike passes outcroppings of the rock, which contrast beautifully with the green of the forest.

The real draw of Hatchet Mountain is the view toward the coast. As you climb, the world opens up before you. Camden Hill, all jagged and irregular, stretches out to the north, and the more rounded domes of Bald and Ragged Mountains rise to the east beyond rolling hills. Below you, at the foot of Hatchet Mountain, Hobbs Pond is a sapphire dropped into the forest.

As you near the summit, atop the last switchback, the view really opens up. You can see rolling country inland from the coastal mountains, and most dramatically, the ocean. Penobscot Bay fills the gap between Mount Megunticook and Bald Mountain. The blue of the water fades into the sky at the horizon line.

A trail leads from this overlook to the wooded summit with its towers and no view. Go to the summit only if you feel the need to stand on the highest ground. Otherwise, stand on the orange rock and look to the sea.

Miles and Directions

0.0   Start from the trailhead behind the gate at the west end of the parking area.

0.7   The trail follows the access road to the tower on the summit, switchbacking up the mountain.

0.8   The trail leaves the access road and climbs to the summit. To complete the hike, return the way you came.

1.6   Arrive back at the trailhead.

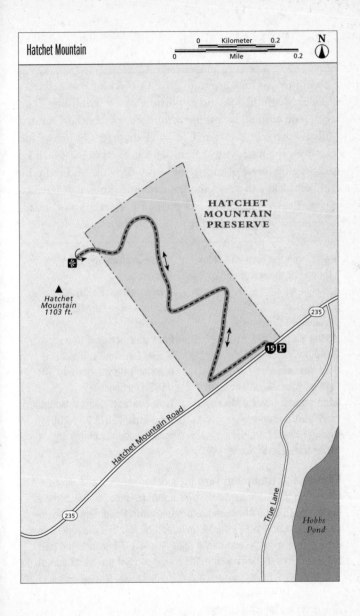

Hatchet Mountain

0 Kilometer 0.2
0 Mile 0.2

N

HATCHET
MOUNTAIN
PRESERVE

Hatchet
Mountain
1103 ft.

235

15 P

Hatchet Mountain Road

235

True Lane

Hobbs
Pond

16 Fernald's Neck

The mostly flat hike around Fernald's Neck offers fine views of Lake Megunticook and opportunities for swimming. The lake is surrounded by mountains, most notably the Camden Hills to the east. Maiden Cliff rises dramatically across the lake from the hike, visible from several viewpoints. The hike is through a forest of mostly old-growth white and red pine and hemlock, and passes the huge boulder known as Balance Rock. Even though this is a popular preserve, you can still have real solitude as you hike through the woods.

Start: From the Fernald's Neck trailhead at the south end of the parking area next to the information sign

Distance: 3.6-mile lollipop

Hiking time: 2 to 3 hours

Difficulty: Moderate

Best season: May–Oct

Trail surface: Woodland path

Land status: Coastal Mountains Land Trust preserve

Nearest town: Camden

Other trail users: None

Water availability: Lake Megunticook

Canine compatibility: Dogs not allowed in Fernald's Neck Preserve

Fees and permits: None

Maps: DeLorme's: The Maine Atlas and Gazetteer: map 14; *USGS Lincolnville*

Trail contact: Coastal Mountains Land Trust, (207) 236-7091; www.coastalmountains.org

Finding the trailhead: From the junction of US 1 and ME 52 (Mountain Street) in Camden, drive north 4.9 miles on ME 52, passing the Maiden Cliff trailhead and Youngstown Road. Turn left onto Fernald's Neck Road. Drive 0.5 mile and bear left at the fork, then drive 0.5 mile to the end of the road. The last 0.1 mile to the parking area is a very narrow lane. The trailhead is at the south end of the parking area next to the Information sign. Trailhead GPS: N44 15.634' / W69 06.578'

The Hike

Lake Megunticook is a long, sinuous lake that lies between Bald Mountain and Mount Megunticook. The lake curls around to the east behind Camden Hills, becoming a series of ponds. Fernald's Neck sticks out into the southern end of the lake, almost bisecting it. The channel on the west side of the neck that connects the southern and northern ends of Lake Megunticook is more like a languid river than a lake.

The hike begins at the end of Fernald's Neck Road in a meadow with views of Maiden Cliff across the lake. The Blue Trail leads into the woods through a forest of old-growth white pine, hemlock, and red pine. The forest stays cool even on the hottest days. Because so little light reaches the ground, little grows beneath the trees; rust-colored needles and cones collect on the trail, hushing your footsteps. There are a few low, mossy spots where the ground is spongy and mosquitoes hang in the air. On the west side of Fernald's Neck, the trail climbs a low, rocky rise that supports blueberries, lichen, and other sun-loving plants. The lake's channel is only 100 feet wide here, the green wall of Bald Mountain rising across the water. The Blue Trail ducks back into the forest and skirts around the Great Bog, where birds and frogs noisily spend their day feeding or defending their territory.

The Orange Trail is a lollipop that loops the rest of the way around Great Bog and toward the southern end of Fernald's Neck. Along the Orange Trail the trees aren't so large, more are spruce, and there is more dead wood beneath the trees. The forest is much less open, but is home to more wildflowers. On the east side of the neck, the trail comes out onto a slab of bedrock that angles down into the lake. Mountain View, as the spot is called, offers fine views of Maiden Cliff and Camden Hills across the lake. This is a popular spot to swim. Boulders stick up out of the lake, offering swimmers spots to sit and relax.

Back on the Blue Trail, the hike heads north to the Yellow Trail. This short trail leads out to another popular swimming spot on the rocky shore. Just behind the shore is Balance Rock, a roughly round boulder the size of a small cabin that sits on the exposed bedrock. It is possible, if you have some rock-climbing skills, to climb atop Balance Rock and stand among the treetops.

Miles and Directions

0.0 Start from the Fernald's Neck trailhead on the Blue Trail next to the information sign.

0.2 The trail passes the White Trail, which gives access to Lake Megunticook, and enters the woods. The Blue Trail forks; go right.

0.4 Pass the Red Trail, staying on the Blue Trail.

0.8 Pass the other end of the Red Trail, staying on the Blue Trail.

1.5 After crossing an open area with views west across a narrow arm of Lake Megunticook, the trail turns inland and goes around the Great Bog. Arrive at the junction with the Orange Trail. Turn right onto the Orange Trail.

1.8 The Orange Trail is a lollipop that loops around the southern end of the preserve. Take the right fork to begin the loop.

2.5 The Orange Trail descends to Lake Megunticook, coming out onto bare rock on the shore. This is Mountain View. Maiden Cliff and Camden Hills are visible across the lake. The trail goes back into the woods at the north end of the rock. (This

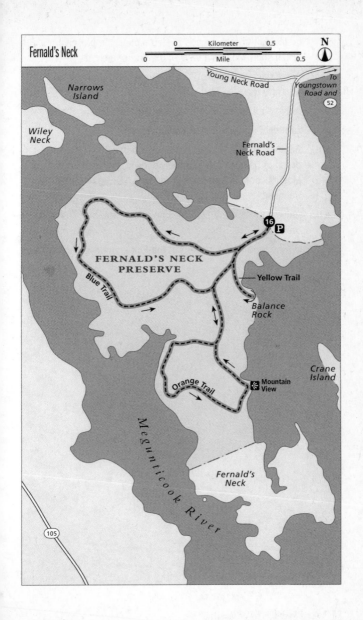

Fernald's Neck

0 Kilometer 0.5
0 Mile 0.5

N

Narrows Island

Wiley Neck

Young Neck Road

To Youngstown Road and 52

Fernald's Neck Road

16 P

FERNALD'S NECK PRESERVE

Yellow Trail

Blue Trail

Balance Rock

Crane Island

Orange Trail

Mountain View

Fernald's Neck

Megunticook River

105

is different from the maps posted around the preserve, which show Mountain View at the end of a short side trail.)

2.7 Arrive back at the fork on the Orange Trail; turn right to return to the Blue Trail.

2.9 Arrive back at the Blue Trail; turn right to continue the hike.

3.0 Turn right onto the Yellow Trail to Balance Rock.

3.2 Balance Rock is a round, cabin-size boulder that sits on a dome of bedrock just into the woods from the shore of Lake Megunticook. Return back to the Blue Trail to return to the trailhead.

3.4 Arrive back at the Blue Trail. Turn right to return to the trailhead.

3.6 On the Blue Trail, turn right at the fork and arrive back at the trailhead.

17 Maiden Cliff

The Maiden Cliff Trail climbs steeply up to the cliffs.
Maiden Cliff offers fine views of the mountains to the west
across Lake Megunticook. To the south, across Camden, the
islands of Penobscot Bay march to the horizon. The hike
continues to the top of Millerite Ridge, with views in every
direction.

Start: From the Maiden Cliff Trail
trailhead at the north end of the
parking area
Distance: 2.1-mile lollipop
Hiking time: About 2 hours
Difficulty: More challenging
Best season: May–Oct
Trail surface: Woodland path
Land status: Town of Camden
parkland
Nearest town: Camden
Other trail users: None

Water availability: Small stream
at miles 0.3 and 1.7
Canine compatibility: Dogs must
be under control at all times
Fees and permits: None
Maps: *DeLorme's The Maine
Atlas and Gazetteer:* map 14;
USGS Lincolnville
Trail contact: Camden Hills
State Park, (207) 236-3109;
www.maine.gov/dacf/parks

Finding the trailhead: From the junction of US 1 and ME 52
(Mountain Street) in Camden, drive north on ME 52 for 2.9 miles.
The trailhead parking is on the right just past the sign for the Lake
Megunticook Beach and Maiden Cliff. The trailhead is at the north
end of the parking area. Trailhead GPS: N44 14.839' / W69 05.272'

The Hike

Maiden Cliff is an escarpment overlooking Lake Megunticook with views of Penobscot Bay out across Camden.
The cliff was named for 12-year-old Elenora French, who

fell 300 feet from the cliff during an 1860's outing and was killed.

Maiden Cliff is on the north ridge of Mount Megunticook, known as Millerite Ridge. It was named for the religious sect that came to believe Jesus' second coming would be on October 22, 1844. The Millerites from Mid-Coast Maine made their way up the north ridge of Mount Megunticook and waited on the open ridgetop. Jesus did not return that day, and the Millerites had to descend the next morning and try to put their lives back together. This event was big news in Camden and across the country, so the ridge came to bear their name.

The trail climbs alongside a small brook that tumbles down the mountainside. Beyond the junction with the Ridge Trail, the Maiden Cliff Trail climbs north, switch-backing up to the cliffs. A cross is at the south end of the cliff, at the point with the most exposure. The cliff runs a distance to the north with a cleft in it. Rough trails run along the cliff top, through the stunted oak trees, allowing you to explore the cliff. Most cliffs in the Camden Hills, like Maiden Cliff, run north–south on the western faces of the mountains.

The Scenic Trail climbs Millerite Ridge from Maiden Cliff, leaving the oaks and entering a maple forest. The open ridgetop offers views in every direction. To the east you can see the open ledge called Zeke's Lookout and the rolling green Camden Hills beyond. Look for blueberries along the trail in late summer.

The Scenic Trail drops off the rocky ridge to a flat area where it ends at the Ridge Trail. This trail follows the ridgetop southeast to the summit of Mount Megunticook. You can also use it to reach Zeke's Trail, which leads farther east across the Camden Hills. The hike turns right, and after

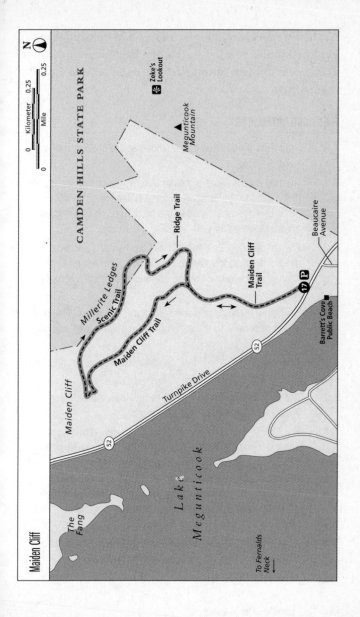

Maiden Cliff

CAMDEN HILLS STATE PARK

Millerite Ledges
Scenic Trail

Maiden Cliff

Ridge Trail

Maiden Cliff Trail

Maiden Cliff Trail

Zeke's
Lookout

Megunticook
Mountain

Turnpike Drive

Beaucaire
Avenue

Barrett's Cove
Public Beach

17 P

Lake
Megunticook

The
Fang

To Fernalds
Neck

N

0   0.25   Kilometer
0   0.25   Mile

one last open view to the west, descends steeply down to the unnamed brook you followed at the beginning of the hike. The brook must be spring fed, because even high on the ridge it runs cold all summer.

Miles and Directions

0.0   Start from the Maiden Cliff trailhead at the north end of the parking area.

0.4   The trail climbs along a stream. After crossing the stream the trail climbs to the junction with the Ridge Trail. You will come down this trail at the end of the hike. Turn left and continue on the Maiden Cliff Trail.

0.9   The Maiden Cliff Trail switchbacks up the ridge and then around to junction with the Scenic Trail. Turn left and hike a short distance out to the top of Maiden Cliff, staying to the left.

1.0   Several unmarked trails wind along the top of the cliffs; they all connect back to the junction of the Maiden Cliff and Scenic Trails.

1.1   Arrive back at the junction. Go straight ahead, east, onto the Scenic Trail.

1.2   The Scenic Trail climbs steeply to the open top of Millerite Ridge, with fine views west and south.

1.5   The Scenic Trail crosses the open ridge, then drops down into the woods to end at the Ridge Trail. If you go straight 1.5 miles on the Ridge Trail, you will reach Megunticook Mountain; you can also use this trail to climb Zeke's Lookout, visible on the ridge to the east, in 1.3 miles. The hike turns right and follows the Ridge Trail west, dropping off the ridge.

1.8   After passing the stream, the Ridge Trail ends at the Maiden Cliff Trail. Turn left and descend to the trailhead.

2.1   Arrive back at the trailhead.

18 Mount Megunticook

Mount Megunticook is the highest of the Camden Hills. The hike to Ocean Lookout on the Mount Megunticook Trail climbs over metamorphic sedimentary rock through a hardwood forest that comes alive with color in the fall. From Ocean Lookout the hike follows the Ridge Trail through a spruce forest to the wooded summit. On the return to the trailhead, you cross Adam's Lookout as you descend the mountain. There are several different trails up Mount Megunticook, and you can extend your hike to include them to reach other mountains such as Mount Battie and Maiden Cliff.

Start: From the north end of the hiker's parking area
Distance: 3.7-mile out-and-back
Hiking time: 2 to 4 hours
Difficulty: More challenging
Best season: May 15–Oct 15
Trail surface: Woodland path
Land status: Camden Hills State Park
Nearest town: Camden
Other trail users: None

Water availability: In the campground and a small stream at mile 1.0
Canine compatibility: Dogs must be on a leash at all times
Fees and permits: State park entrance fee
Maps: *DeLorme's: The Maine Atlas and Gazetteer:* map 14; *USGS Camden*
Trail contact: Camden Hills State Park, (207) 236-3109, www.maine.gov/dacf/parks

Finding the trailhead: From the junction of US 1 and ME 52 (Mountain Road) in Camden, drive north on US 1 for 1.6 miles. Turn left into the Camden Hills State Park entrance. Before the entrance gate, turn left into the hiker's parking area. The trailhead is 0.2 mile up the road in the campground. Pay your entrance fee at the gate and walk into the campground. Stay straight ahead through the campground. The trailhead is on the left; there is a sign for Mount Megunticook. Trailhead GPS: N44 13.934' / W69 03.170'

The Hike

Mount Megunticook, at 1,385 feet, is the highest of the Camden Hills. Its summit ridge runs northwest to southeast from Maiden Cliff to Ocean Lookout. This hike climbs to Ocean Lookout and on to the wooded summit. The mountain's name is a corruption of the Native American name for Camden Harbor and roughly means "big mountain harbor." This hike uses the shortest and most direct of the several hiking routes up the mountain. There are many ways to combine this hike with climbs of other mountains in the western park of Camden Hills State Park. Once you hike away from Ocean Lookout, you are unlikely to see another hiker, even on a sunny summer day.

The Camden Hills are knobs of very hard metamorphic rock. The tectonic action that resulted in the volcanic eruptions that created much of the Downeast coastal bedrock ground sand and gravel on the continental shelf into very hard, weather-resistant rock. As you hike up the Mount Megunticook Trail, notice how many different colors and textures of rock there are. Unlike the rather uniform granites of Mount Desert Island, the bedrock on Mount Megunticook reflects the diversity of the rock that was metamorphosed into these hills. Their hardness allowed them to resist the grinding of the glaciers, leaving rounded, rocky mountains.

The hike climbs through a hardwood forest that is alive with color in the fall, making it one of the best fall hikes in the region. Above Ocean Lookout, the Ridge Trail passes

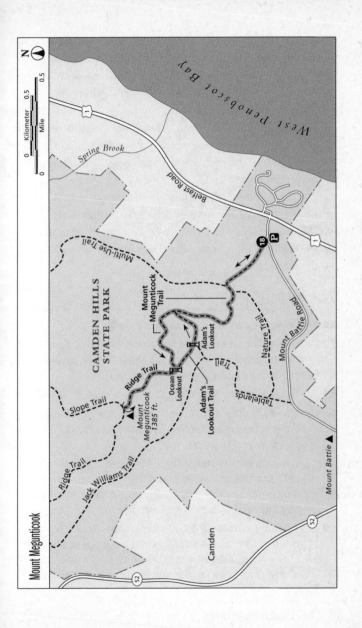

Mount Megunticook

through a spruce forest. The hike to the summit is well worth the effort—even though there are no views to be had—just to walk through this quiet green woods. Along the way be sure to look for lady slipper orchids and other wildflowers that like acidic soils.

From Ocean Lookout you can see the coast from Owl's Head to Castine and Penobscot Bay dotted with islands. The two long irregular islands, North Haven and Vinalhaven, are in the foreground inland.

The hike follows the Ridge Trail down along the edge of the cliffs to the Adam's Lookout Trail. Continuing down would eventually take you across Mount Battie and on into Camden. Follow the Adam's Lookout Trail east to the Mount Megunticook Trail.

Miles and Directions

0.0 Begin at the north end of the hiker's parking area.

0.2 Walk up the park road into the campground, stopping to pay the entrance fee at the gate. Stay straight ahead through the campground to the Multi-Use Trail on the left.

0.3 Turn left onto the Mount Megunticook Trail.

0.9 Mount Megunticook Trail climbs, then turns east to a junction with the Adam's Lookout Trail. Continue straight on the Mount Megunticook Trail.

1.4 The trail climbs on rock slabs beside a small stream, then turns south away from the stream. The trail comes out onto the open ledges known as Ocean Lookout, where the Mount Megunticook Trail ends at the Ridge Trail.

1.9 To reach Mount Megunticook's summit from Ocean Lookout, hike north on the Ridge Trail. The trail winds through a spruce forest. Just before the summit, which is marked with a large cairn, is the junction with the Slope Trail. (**Option:**

You can hike another 2.1 miles from here to Maiden Cliff.)
To continue the hike, retrace your steps back to Ocean
Lookout.

2.4 Arrive back at Ocean Lookout.

2.5 Continue south on the Ridge Trail, descending along the cliff
edge. Arrive at the junction with the Adam's Lookout Trail.
Turn left onto the Adam's Lookout Trail.

2.6 Arrive at Adam's Lookout.

2.8 Arrive back at the Mount Megunticook Trail. Turn right to
retrace your steps back to the trailhead and hiker's parking
area.

3.7 Arrive back at the hiker's parking area.

19 Bald Rock Mountain

The open rock summit of Bald Rock Mountain, has views as fine as any in the Camden Hills, yet you are unlikely to see another hiker on the trail. From the summit you have a sweeping view of Penobscot Bay and its islands. Beyond the bay you can see Blue Hill and the mountains of Mount Desert Island.

Start: From the Multi-Use Trailhead at the south end of the parking area
Distance: 3.4-mile lollipop
Hiking time: About 3 to 4 hours
Difficulty: More challenging
Best season: May–Oct
Trail surface: Gravel road and woodland path
Land Status: Camden Hills State Park
Nearest Town: Lincolnville

Other trail users: The Multi-Use Trail is open to bicycles
Water availability: None
Canine compatibility: Dogs must be on a leash at all times
Fees and permits: None
Maps: *DeLorme's The Maine Atlas and Gazetteer* map 14; *USGS Lincolnville*
Trail Contact: Camden Hills State Park, (207) 236-3109, www.maine.gov/dacf/parks

Finding the trailhead: From downtown Camden drive north 5.9 miles on US 1. Turn left onto ME 173. Drive 2.2 miles on ME 173. Turn left onto Youngtown Road and immediately turn left again into the trailhead parking area. Trailhead GPS: N44 16.797' / W69 02.692'

The Hike

The Multi-Use Trail—really a gravel road closed to auto traffic—cuts all the way across the Camden Hills to the main park entrance. Follow the trail as it gradually climbs southeast through towering hardwoods, mostly maple.

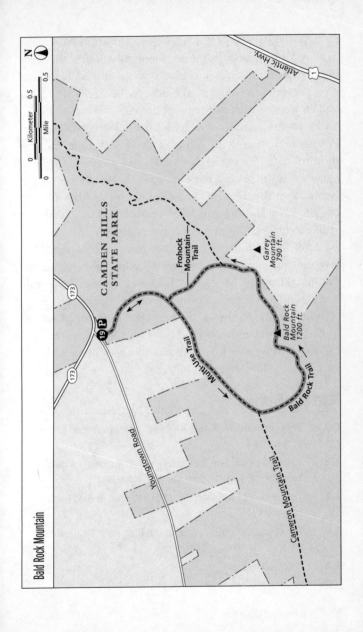

Bald Rock Mountain

The Bald Rock Trail climbs away from the Multi-Use Trail and into a rocky evergreen forest. As you near the summit, the mature evergreens give way to stunted birch and spruce, exposed bedrock, and blueberry bushes. A short side trail climbs the rock to the open summit.

From the summit you have an unobstructed view of Penobscot Bay with Islesboro in the foreground. You can sit in solitude munching blueberries and watching the ferry chug across the open water between Lincolnville Beach and Islesboro. In the distance, across the jumble of islands in the bay, Blue Hill and the mountains of Mount Desert Island are visible as blue–gray outlines on the horizon.

After filling yourself with blueberries and the view, follow the trail northeast from where you clambered to the summit. The trail passes two backpacking lean-tos before descending past interesting rock formations. The trail drops steeply into the hardwood forest to the Frohock Mountain Trail. Turn right and you head out over Derry Mountain to Frohock Mountain. Turn left and descend along a stream back to the Multi-Use Trail.

Miles and Directions

0.0 Begin from the Multi-Use Trailhead at the south end of the parking area.

1.2 Follow the Multi-Use Trail, climbing gently through a hardwood forest. Turn left onto the Bald Rock Trail.

1.9 Turn right onto the short trail to the summit of Bald Rock Mountain.

2.0 To complete the hike, return to the Bald Rock Trail and turn right.

2.1 Pass two lean-tos.

2.6 The Bald Rock Trail ends at a T intersection. Turn left onto the Frohock Mountain Trail.

2.9 Arrive back at the Multi-Use Trail. Turn right to return to the trailhead.

3.4 Arrive back at the trailhead.

20 Tanglewood

This hike loops around the perimeter of Tanglewood, a 4–H camp within Camden Hills State Park. The trails are through a towering oak–pine forest and along the Ducktrap River. The woods feel much more remote than they are; you might even see an eagle along the river.

Start: From the trailhead next to the Information sign
Distance: 4.5-mile loop
Hiking time: About 3 to 4 hours
Difficulty: Moderate
Best season: May–Oct
Trail surface: Woodland path
Land Status: University of Maine's Tanglewood 4-H Camp located within Camden Hills State Park
Nearest Town: Lincolnville
Other trail users: The trails are popular with cross-country skiers; no other users during the rest of the year
Water availability: Ducktrap River and Black Brook
Canine compatibility: Dogs must be on a leash at all times
Fees and permits: None
Maps: *DeLorme's The Maine Atlas and Gazetteer* map 14; *USGS Lincolnville*
Trail contact: Camden Hills State Park, (207) 236-3109, www.maine.gov/dacf/parks

Finding the trailhead: From the junction of US 1 and ME 173 Lincolnville, drive north on US 1 for 1.0 mile. Turn left onto Ducktrap Road. Drive 0.7 mile to Tanglewood Road. Turn right onto Tanglewood Road. Drive 0.9 mile to the trailhead parking area. There is parking on both sides of Tanglewood Road; the trailhead is on the left side of the road. Trailhead GPS: N44 18.147' / W69 01.949'

The Hike

Tanglewood is a 4-H camp run by the University of Maine in Camden Hills State Park. The land is low rolling woods along the Ducktrap River north of the actual Camden Hills. The hike follows trails around the perimeter of Tanglewood through a forest of mature oaks and pines. Beneath the trees, wildflowers and especially ferns abound. Because the trails are popular in the winter with cross-country skiers, the trail is mostly level and wide. There are a number of low spots that can be swampy in spring or after heavy rains.

The hike follows the Ducktrap River upstream for 1.6 miles, a narrow stream no more than 20 feet across. It winds sinuously through the woods. At first it is a shallow stream, noisily running across cobbles and low ledges. As you hike upstream, the river becomes deeper with a mud bed. A small river like this may not seem the place, but be on the lookout for eagles.

The muddy streambed is the result of the metamorphic and sedimentary bedrock that the stream passes over. The harder metamorphic rock becomes cobbles in sections of the riverbed and occasional boulders that sit in the stream. At the 4-H camp there is a muddy pool in a wide bend in the river that looks like it once was used for swimming. Please stay on the trail along this section and leave the camp to the campers. Along the Nature Trail, upstream from this pool, the river runs alongside a low outcropping of metamorphic bedrock. All along the river its calm surface reflects the trees that hang out over the water, trying to close the canopy over the river.

At mile 2.5, the trail leaves the Ducktrap River and follows Black Brook upstream. This little stream is much like the Ducktrap River, only smaller and more sinuous. It runs through low wet woods. As the trail leaves the stream, you hike back into the towering oak–pine forest, passing several trails before arriving back at the trailhead.

Miles and Directions

0.0   Start from the trailhead next to the Information sign.

0.1   The Forest Loop Trail forks; take the right fork. The left fork is where the hike ends.

0.7   The Forest Loop Trail crosses Tanglewood Road, then goes north toward the Ducktrap River. Turn right onto the River Trail.

0.9   Just before the river, you come to a junction with the Turner Falls Trail. This trail follows the river downstream toward Penobscot Bay. Turn left and head upstream along the Ducktrap River on the River Trail.

1.8   Arrive at the junction with the Forest Loop Trail. For the next 0.2 mile the two trails are the same. Go straight, staying along the river.

1.9   Arrive at the junction with the Pitcher Pond Trail. To the right on the trail is a snowmobile bridge across the Duck-trap River. Continue straight on the River Trail, passing the Tanglewood Museum. The camp staff asks that you stay on the trails and away from the camp itself.

2.0   Turn right onto the Nature Trail. The camp village is just south along Tanglewood Road.

2.5   The Nature Trail goes around a small pool and then continues to follow the Ducktrap River upstream. The Nature Trail turns southeast away from the river. Go straight onto the River Trail, which heads southwest away from the river.

2.6   The River Trail ends at the Forest Loop Trail. Turn right onto the Forest Loop Trail, which follows along Black Brook.

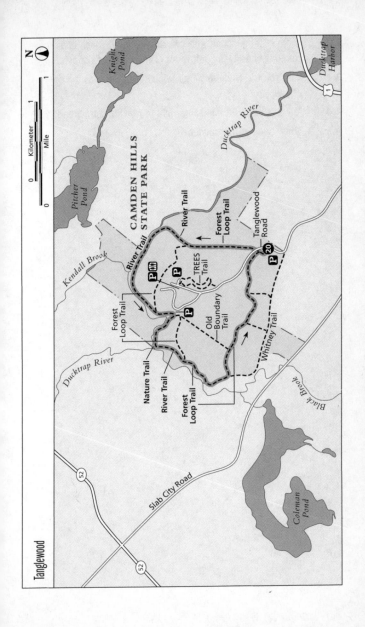

Tanglewood

3.2   Arrive at the junction with the Whitney Trail, which is a cross-country ski trail. Turn left to stay on the Forest Loop Trail.

3.4   Pass the Old Boundary Trail, which goes north to the camp village.

4.4   Arrive back at the fork. Turn right to reach the trailhead.

4.5   Arrive back at the trailhead.

21 Knight Pond

Knight Pond is nestled in a quiet valley between Ducktrap Mountain and rolling hills to the north. The hike leads along the shore to a rocky point covered with mature white pines. You then hike back through the woods on the shoulder of Ducktrap Mountain to the trail system of the Point Lookout Resort. There is a small sand beach near the trailhead.

Start: From the trail that leaves the west side of the boat launch at the south end of Knight Pond
Distance: 1.5-mile loop
Hiking time: About 1 to 2 hours
Difficulty: Moderate
Best season: May–Oct
Trail surface: Woodland path
Land status: The hike passes through or near lands owned by the town of Northport, the Coastal Mountains Land Trust, and Point Lookout Resort
Nearest Town: Northport
Other trail users: None
Water availability: Knight Pond

Canine compatibility: Dogs must be on a leash at all times
Fees and permits: Point Lookout Resort asks that hikers visit the reception desk at the resort off US 1 in Lincolnville to sign in and pay a trail-use fee
Maps: *DeLorme's The Maine Atlas and Gazetteer* map 14; *USGS Isleboro*
Trail contact: Coastal Mountains Land Trust, (207) 236-7091, www.coastalmountains.org; Point Lookout Resort, (207) 789-2000, www.visitpointlookout.com

Finding the trailhead: From downtown Camden drive north 11.2 miles on US 1. Turn left onto Beech Hill Road, just past Wentworth Family Grocery. Drive 2.4 miles. Turn left onto Knight's Pond Road. Drive 1.8 miles to the end of the road. The trailhead is on the west side of the boat ramp that leads into the south end of the pond. Trailhead GPS: N44 18.817' / W68° 59.695'

The Hike

Knight's Pond Road ends at a boat ramp. To the right of the boat ramp is a small sand beach at the end of Knight Pond. To the left, a trail leads along the south shore of the pond to a pine-covered point. You can walk out onto the bedrock and see Ducktrap Mountain rising to the south across a swampy bay full of lily pads. Across the lake, wooded hills roll down to the pond's shore. Open patches with barns and farmhouses dot the hills. Dragonflies buzz around and frogs croak among the lily pads.

From the point follow the inland trail back to the east, turning uphill away from the pond at the junction. The Knights Pond Trail climbs gently through tall pines. Turn right onto Moosehead Trail at the junction. This trail climbs and then levels out in the deeply shaded forest. Turn right onto Megunticook Trail and soon emerge from the forest onto a wide grass cross-country ski trail.

This trail also climbs, looping around to Point Lookout Drive. You can continue hiking across the road and climbing to the resort at Point Lookout. Or you can lounge on the lawn, looking out toward Penobscot Bay before returning to the Megunticook Trail and the quiet woods.

When you get back to Moosehead Trail, continue straight on the Megunticook Trail to Knights Pond Trail, which will take you back to the trailhead.

Miles and Directions

0.0 Start from the trail on the west side of the boat ramp down into Knight Pond.

0.2 Follow the trail along the shore of Knight Pond to where it ends on a rocky point covered with large white pines.

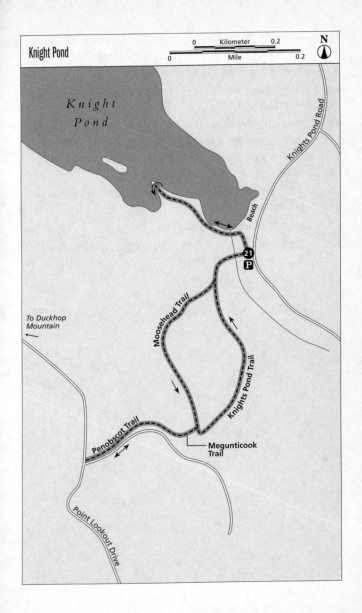

Knight Pond

Knight Pond

Knights Pond Road

Beach

21 **P**

Moosehead Trail

To Duckhop Mountain

Knights Pond Trail

Penobscot Trail

Megunticook Trail

Point Lookout Drive

Kilometer

0   0.2

Mile

0   0.2

N

0.5 Return on the more inland Knights Pond Trail. Turn right onto the Moosehead Trail at the junction with a sign.

0.7 Turn right onto the Megunticook Trail.

0.8 The Megunticook Trail ends at the wide grassy Penobscot Trail. Turn right.

0.9 Reach Lookout Point Drive. To complete the hike, retrace your steps to the Megunticook Trail. (**Option:** You can continue straight ahead, climbing to Lookout Point with fine views.)

1.0 Arrive back at the Megunticook Trail. Turn left and reenter the woods.

1.1 Cross the Moosehead Trail.

1.2 The Megunticook Trail ends at the Knights Pond Trail. Turn left to return to the trailhead.

1.5 Arrive back at the trailhead.

22 The Canal Path

The Canal Path is a self-guided hike along the St. George River past a long-abandoned section of canal in a working pine forest. There are information signs along the trail that show you where the canal and its locks once were. The trail loops around the inside of a wide bend in the river through maples.

Start: From the trailhead next to the kiosk and across the St. George River from the parking area

Distance: 2.4-mile out-and-back

Hiking time: About 2 to 3 hours

Difficulty: Easy

Best season: May–Oct

Trail surface: Woodland path

Land status: Robbins Lumber woodlands

Nearest town: Searsmont

Other trail users: None

Water availability: The St. George River

Canine compatibility: Dogs need to be on a leash at all times

Fees and permits: None

Maps: *DeLorme's The Maine Atlas and Gazetteer* map 14; *USGS Searsmont*

Trail contact: The Georges River Land Trust, (207) 594-5166, www.GeorgesRiver.org

Finding the trailhead: From downtown Camden drive north 11.4 miles on ME 105. Turn right onto ME 131 and drive 1.7 miles. Turn right onto Ghent Road. Drive 0.4 mile, across the St. George River. Parking is in a gravel lot on the right. The trailhead is across the river, next to the kiosk. Trailhead GPS: N44 20.133' / W69 11.944'

The Hike

In 1793 Charles Barrett began building a canal system from Lake St. George along the St. George River to tidewater in Thomaston to carry timber and farm goods. It was one of the first canal systems in the United States. He sold the unfinished canal to Henry Knox (for whom Knox County is named). The canal was never completed and fell into disuse because of the expense of building the canal and the derth of goods that traveled on it. When Knox died in 1806, the canal system was abandoned.

In the 1840s—during the height of the national canal boom—the lower 28-mile section of the canal was rebuilt to haul lumber from the Robbins Mill. This canal was made obsolete by the railroad and abandoned in 1877.

The Canal Path follows the St. George River where part of the canal infrastructure is visible in the forest beside the river. There are informational signs along the hike with maps and text that show you where locks and dams were. The trail follows the still-visible canal channel for a short section.

The trail then loops around a wide bend in the river through an open maple forest, passing a side trail that leads out through tall grass. This trail follows the river south 1.6 miles to ME 105, ending across the road from the Appleton Preserve.

On your return hike along the canal route, take time to enjoy the wild river and shady forest dominated by mature white pines. Even without the canal history, this would be a fine hike.

Miles and Directions

0.0 Start from the kiosk at the edge of the field near the St. George River.

0.9 The trail follows the river, passing the first five points on the self-guided trail and several historical markers. Go straight at the fork in the trail.

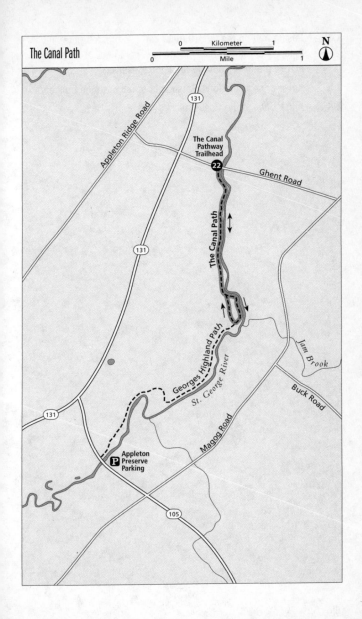

The Canal Path

Kilometer
0   1
Mile
0   1

N

131

Appleton Ridge Road

The Canal
Pathway
Trailhead

22

Ghent Road

The Canal Path

131

Georges Highland Path

St. George River

Jam Brook

Buck Road

131

Magog Road

Appleton
Preserve
Parking

P

105

1.1   Pass a trail on the left. (**Option:** You can turn left here and follow this trail 1.6 miles along the river to ME 105, ending across the road from the Appleton Preserve.)

1.5   Arrive back at the fork. Go straight to return to the trailhead.

2.4   Arrive back at the trailhead.

23 Frye Mountain

Frye Mountain lies across the headwaters of Bartlett Stream, which feeds the St. George River through Quantabacook Lake. The hike follows the northernmost section of the Georges Highland Path to the mountain's mostly wooded summit. While the hike offers no great vistas, it is a relatively easy hike through a variety of forest types with a possibility of seeing wildlife.

Start: From where the Georges Highland Path crosses Walker Ridge Road
Distance: 6.4-mile out-and-back
Hiking time: About 3 to 4 hours
Difficulty: More challenging
Best season: May–Oct
Trail surface: Woodland path
Land status: Frye Mountain State Game Management Area
Nearest town: Liberty
Other trail users: Frye Mountain is open to hunting in season; there are several ATV trails that cross the Georges Highland Path on this hike
Water availability: Bartlett Stream at mile 0.3
Canine compatibility: Dogs must be under control at all times
Fees and permits: None
Maps: *DeLorme's The Maine Atlas and Gazetteer* map 14; *USGS Morrill and Liberty*
Trail contact: Maine Department of Inland Fisheries & Wildlife, www.maine.gov/ifw

Finding the trailhead: From downtown Camden drive north 11.4 miles on ME 105. Turn right onto ME 131 and drive 3.4 miles. Turn left onto ME 173 and drive 7.2 miles. Go straight onto ME 220. Drive 4.3 miles to Bean's Corner, where there is a large sign with distances to various Maine towns. Bear left, staying on ME 220. Drive 1.1 miles. Turn right onto Walker Ridge Road. Drive past the state garage and up the hill 0.2 mile. Look for blue flagging in trees on both sides of the road. This is where the Georges Highland Path crosses the road. There are also small wooden signs that read GHP. The trailhead is on the right side of the road. Trailhead GPS: N44 28.509' / W69 15.119'

The Hike

This hike follows the Georges Highland Path (GHP) from Walker Ridge Road to its northern terminus on the summit of Frye Mountain within Frye Mountain Wildlife Management Area. From the trailhead the GHP descends gently through a hardwood forest to Bartlett Stream. This stream flows through Quantabacook Lake in Searsmont to the St. George River, making Frye Mountain one of the river's headwaters.

Bartlett Stream winds beneath high banks through a shady evergreen forest dominated by large hemlocks. A high-water trail offers an alternative to fording the stream—only necessary in the spring. The trail follows the stream, then turns south toward Pierce Hill, passing through various forest types. Stone walls that run through the regenerating forest and an old road are reminders that not long ago this was farmland. Much of the forest is open, and the trail is little used. Without the frequent blue blazes, you would easily lose the trail. It feels like you are making your own trail where no one else has gone.

The trail turns east and then north, beginning to climb the western flank of Frye Mountain, reaching a junction below the mountain's open shoulder. Turn left, hiking along the northern flank of the mountain. The trail passes over three semi-open areas along Frye Mountain's long summit ridge. You have limited views through the treetops. Surprisingly, you see more stone walls along the ridgeline, suggesting the mountain had been cleared to its summit.

After a short, steep climb you reach the semi-open summit. The opening is large enough to have blueberry

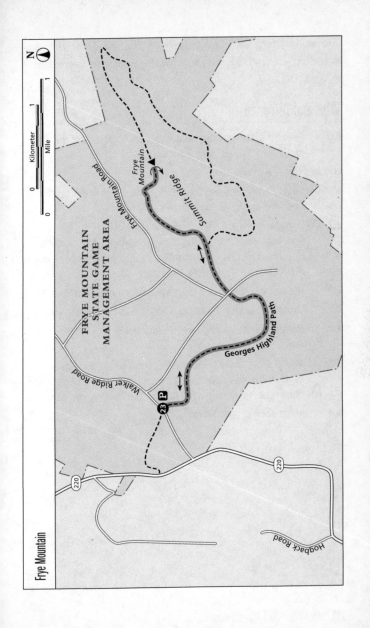

Frye Mountain

bushes, but it is too small to offer any views of the surrounding country. This hike is for enjoying the journey, not its destination.

Miles and Directions

0.0   Follow the Georges Highland Path east (right side of the road) from Walker Ridge Road.

100 feet Pass an information kiosk.

0.3   Cross Bartlett Stream. There is a marked high-water trail for when the stream is too high to safely ford.

2.1   The trail reaches a junction on the shoulder of Frye Mountain. Turn left to hike to the summit. (**Option:** The trail to the right loops around Frye Mountain, returning to this point in 4.5 miles.)

2.3   The trail crosses a semi-open knob with limited views.

2.7   The trail crosses a larger semi-open knob with limited views.

3.0   The trail crosses a small rocky outcropping with limited views.

3.2   After a short, steep climb the trail reaches the semi-open summit. The unmarked summit is at the east end of the open area. To complete the hike, return the way you came.

6.4   Arrive back at the trailhead.

24 Hogback Mountain

This hike follows the Georges Highland Path west from ME 220 to the summit of Hogback Mountain. The trail first climbs Hogback Ledges, then contours south around the ledges through a forest dominated by beech to a spring. Beyond the spring, the trail leaves the forest and follows a dirt logging road. The trail reenters the forest and climbs across a false summit then to the open ledges near the summit. The trail loops across the summit and back to the logging road.

Start: From the west side of ME 220 where the Georges Highland Path crosses the road

Distance: 3.9-mile lollipop

Hiking time: About 2 to 4 hours

Difficulty: More challenging

Best season: May–Oct

Trail surface: Woodland path and logging road

Land status: Georges Highland Path through private property

Nearest town: Liberty

Other trail users: Hunting is permitted in season; there may be some logging activity

Water availability: The trail passes a spring at mile 0.7

Canine compatibility: Dogs need to be under control at all times

Fees and permits: None

Maps: *DeLorme's The Maine Atlas and Gazetteer* map 14; *USGS Liberty*

Trail contact: Georges River Land Trust, www.grlt.org

Finding the trailhead: From downtown Camden drive north 11.4 miles on ME 105. Turn right onto ME 131 and drive 3.4 miles. Turn left onto ME 173 and drive 7.2 miles. Go straight onto ME 220. Drive 4.3 miles to Bean's Corner, where there is a large sign with distances to various Maine towns. Bear left, staying on ME 220. Drive 1.1 miles. On the right is Walker Ridge Road, and on the left is the Montville Gravel Pit. Continue on ME 220 for 0.3 mile. The trailhead is on the left side of the road. On the right side of the road is a square of blue-painted plywood. You can park on the shoulder on either side of the road. Trailhead GPS: N44 28.513' / W69 15.715'

The Hike

The Georges Highland Path crosses a wet area on bog boards, then climbs to Hogback Ledges through mature pines. The trail contours to the south around the mountain, going up and down through a beech forest and passing several erratics. The trail climbs along a small braided stream to where a spring spills over a natural rock wall. Even in summer the water is crisp and cool.

The trail crosses a swampy area above the rock wall formed by the spring and through the woods to a dirt logging road at the edge of a recent cut. Follow the road to the left, climbing to a junction with a trail sign. Turn left and reenter the woods.

The trail climbs through hardwoods to a semi-open false summit. Follow the blue blazes down and back into the woods. The trail here is in deep, cool shade through a mixed forest. After a short easy climb, the trail reaches open ledges with fine views from southwest to east. You can see Lake Megunticook and the Camden Hills in the distance.

The trail turns north and crosses Hogback Mountain's unmarked summit. The trail winds through mature evergreens with an understory mostly of rocks and moss, with limited views north. The trail descends through hardwoods, mostly birch, to a junction with the Hogback Connector. This trail leads west into Sheepscot Headwaters trail network. Turn right and follow an old woods road back to the marked junction at the edge of the cut.

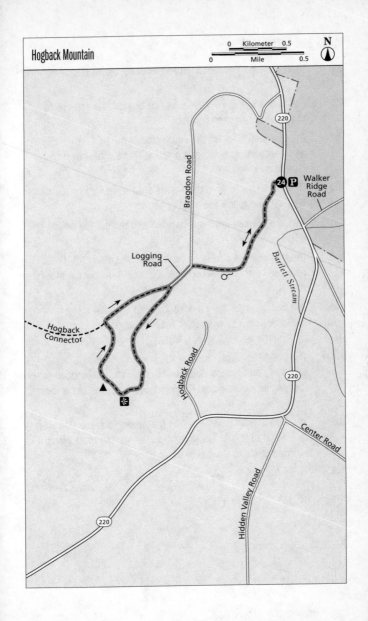

Hogback Mountain

0   Kilometer   0.5
0   Mile   0.5

N

Bragdon Road

220

24 P Walker Ridge Road

Logging Road

Bartlett Stream

Hogback Connector

Hogback Road

220

220

Center Road

Hidden Valley Road

Miles and Directions

0.0   Start from the Georges Highland Path on the west side of ME 220.

0.3   The trail crosses a wet area on bog boards, then climbs to the base of Hogback Ledges.

0.7   The trail slabs around the south side of the ridge, climbing and descending, arriving at a spring that tumbles over a natural rock wall.

0.9   The trail emerges from the woods onto a dirt logging road. Turn left and follow the road uphill.

1.1   Reach a marked junction. Turn left and reenter the woods on a trail.

1.3   The trail crosses a false summit. There are many ATV trails between here and the overlook. Be sure to follow the blue blazes.

1.9   The trail emerges from the woods onto an open rocky overlook. (**Option:** You can return the way you came from here, making the hike 0.2 mile shorter.)

2.4   The trail bears right, crossing the unmarked summit, and wanders north across Hogback Mountain to the junction with the Hogback Connector. Turn right and follow an old woods road.

2.8   The woods road drops down to the marked intersection you passed at mile 1.1. Go straight on the logging road, retracing your steps to the trailhead.

3.9   Arrive back at the trailhead.

25 Sears Island

Sears Island has been used by humans for centuries, and in the last century all kinds of development schemes threatened the island. But today most of it is protected by a conservation easement. The hike goes through the protected lands along mostly flat trails. You have opportunities to see and hike through a large number of habitat types. The hike can be altered to take in some of the numerous unmarked trails that criss-cross the island or a walk along the rocky shore.

Start: From steps down to the beach to the left of the Information sign beyond the barricades
Distance: 4.3-mile out-and-back
Hiking time: About 2 to 3 hours
Difficulty: Moderate
Best season: May–Oct; the island is most popular during spring and fall bird migration
Trail surface: Woodland trail, two track lane, and road walk
Land status: State land with Friends of Sears Island conservation easement

Nearest town: Searsport
Other trail users: Bikers, birders, and hunters
Water availability: None
Canine compatibility: Dogs need to be under control at all times
Fees and permits: None
Maps: DeLorme's *The Maine Atlas and Gazetteer* map 15; *USGS Searsport* and *Castine*
Trail contact: Friends of Sears Island, (855) 884-2284, friendsofsearsisland.org

Finding the trailhead: From Searsport drive north 2.1 miles on US 1. Turn right onto Sears Island Road; there is a sign for the preserve. The road ends in 1.0 mile across the causeway. Park along the road or in the gravel lot on the left. The trailhead is beyond the barricades on the left side of Jetty Road at the Information sign. Trailhead GPS: N44 27.425' / W68 52.932'

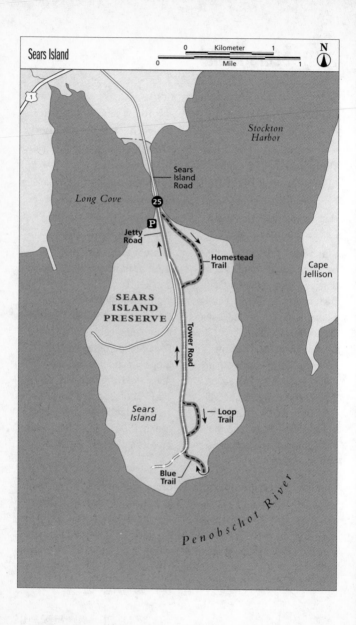

Sears Island

0 · Kilometer · 1
0 · Mile · 1

N

Stockton Harbor

①

Long Cove

Sears Island Road

25

P

Jetty Road

Homestead Trail

Cape Jellison

SEARS ISLAND PRESERVE

Tower Road

Sears Island

Loop Trail

Blue Trail

Penobschot River

The Hike

People have been using Sears Island for centuries. The Penobscots fished from the sandbar that connects the island to the mainland. There have been several farms on the island. As you hike you can see evidence of fields and buildings, mostly along the Homestead Trail. A few cellar holes remain, and the checkerboard of forest types and ages on the island show where homesites, fields, and pastures once were. The island, especially the northeast quarter, is crisscrossed with stone walls built from erratic granite stones. Over time these walls begin to look like a natural part of the woods, as the walls collapse and the stones become encrusted with lichen and moss. In several places, especially along the Homestead Trail near Tower Road, the woods were once orchards. Apple trees still grow beneath the taller forest, leaving petals scattered on the ground in the late spring that attract deer.

In the 1970s plans were put forward to use the island as a major port or site of a nuclear power plant. More recently, a paved road was built to and across the island as part of a development scheme that included a liquified natural gas terminal. None of those happened, in part because of the popularity of the island with birders and hikers. Since 2009 about two thirds of the island, now owned by the state, is protected by a conservation easement. The conserved lands are mostly on the eastern half of the island.

The island is not wilderness, but it is wild enough to support deer and coyotes. Moose have even been seen on the island. Its waters support seals, osprey, and eagles. In other words, Sears Island is not wilderness, but it is getting wilder all the time.

The island has numerous unmarked trails that wander across and around it. This hike follows the few marked and maintained trails. It accesses the shore at the beginning and at the end of the Blue Trail. One alternative hike would be to follow the trails to the end of the Blue Trail and then walk back to the trailhead along the beach up the east side of the island. The waters at the head of Penobscot Bay and between Sears Island and Cape Jellison are good habitat for eagles and harbor seals.

Miles and Directions

0.0   Start at the Information sign beyond the barricade south of the parking area. The paved Jetty Road goes south; the Homestead Trail begins down the stairs to the left of the sign. Take the stairs.

0.1   The Homestead Trail goes into the woods at the sign along the shore.

0.8   The Homestead Trail ends at Tower Road. Turn left and hike down the gravel two track.

1.6   Turn left down the Loop Trail.

1.9   The Loop Trail ends at Tower Road. Turn left and hike south on Tower Road.

2.0   Turn left onto the Blue Trail. If you came to a closeable gate on Tower Road, you passed the Blue Trail.

2.3   The Blue Trail descends through a ferny woods to the shore where it ends. You can explore the shoreline all the way around the island. To continue the hike, return to the Tower Road.

2.6   Arrive back at Tower Road. Turn right and follow the two-track back toward the trailhead.

2.7   Pass the Loop Trail.

2.9   Pass the Loop Trail.

3.7 Pass the Homestead Trail.

3.9 Tower Road ends at the paved Jetty Road. To hike back to the trailhead, turn right.

4.3 Arrive back at the trailhead.

26 Fort Point State Park

More than a hike, this is a stroll around Fort Point. You walk through the site of Fort Pownal on your way to the shore where the lighthouse is perched atop a high bluff overlooking the mouth of the Penobscot River. The walk continues northwest along the shore to the end of the bluff where you can walk out of a gravel spit. The trail then passes through a wooded picnic area to a historic pier, then back to the trailhead.

Start: From the kiosk in the grassy meadow to the south of the parking area
Distance: 0.9 mile loop
Hiking time: About 1 to 2 hours
Difficulty: Easy
Best season: May–Oct
Trail surface: Woodland path and mown meadow
Land status: Fort Point State Park
Nearest town: Stockton Springs
Other trail users: None

Water availability: None
Canine compatibility: Dogs must be on a leash at all times
Fees and permits: There is a state park entrance fee, payable at the self-service gate at the park entrance
Maps: *DeLorme's The Maine Atlas and Gazetteer* map 15: *USGS Castine*
Trail contact: Fort Point State Park, (207) 941-4014, www .maine.gov/fortpoint

Finding the trailhead: From downtown Camden, drive 28.8 miles north on US 1 to Stockton Springs. Turn right onto Main Street at Just Barb's Restaurant. Drive 0.7 mile. Turn right onto Cape Jellison Road at the sign for Fort Point State Park. Drive 0.9 mile to a fork. Turn left, staying on Cape Jellison Road. Drive 1.5 miles to the park entrance. Turn left into the park at the large wooded sign. Drive 1.0 mile to the parking area on the right, passing the fee station. The trailhead is at the kiosk in the mowed meadow south of the first parking area. Trailhead GPS: N44 28.122' / W68 48.712'

The Hike

The walk begins by passing through the site of Fort Pownal. In May 1759, Massachusetts Governor Thomas Pownall came here with an army to build a fort at the mouth of the Penobscot River, which at the time was part of Massachusetts. The fort was designed to protect English settlers in the region from both the French and the Indians, who had been using the area for centuries. The governor named the fort after himself, but somehow in the last two and a half centuries the final L in the name has been lost.

After the British removed the cannons and abandoned the fort in 1775, colonists overran and destroyed the fort. Today its outline can be seen on the ground, but no evidence of the fort itself exists. Interpretive signs around the site help you visualize the fort in your mind.

Atop a high bluff along the mouth of the Penobscot River, sits a white lighthouse and its bell tower. This was the first river light built in Maine. At the time, at the head of tide up the Penobscot River, Bangor was one of the busiest American seaports, shipping lumber to the world. The light protected this important waterway.

Farther along the shore, you can walk out onto a gravel bar. It looks like a good place for swimming, but the park asks that you stay out of the water. Swirling currents on the incoming and outgoing tides make the water hazardous. From the gravel bar, you can see the water swirling in fast eddies as it rushes by.

A trail leads north through a wooded picnic area to a pier on the site of a historic pier. From the pier you have a fine

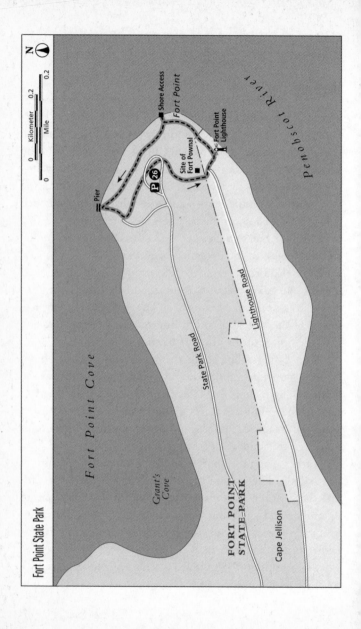

Fort Point State Park

N

Fort Point Cove

Grant's Cove

Pier

P 26

Site of Fort Pownal

Shore Access

Fort Point

Fort Point Lighthouse

Penobscot River

State Park Road

Lighthouse Road

FORT POINT STATE PARK

Cape Jellison

Kilometer 0 0.2
Mile 0 0.2

view of Fort Point Cove and the Penobscot River below Verona Island. Across the river is the town of Castine.

Miles and Directions

0.0 Start from the kiosk in the mowed field south of the parking area.

0.1 Cross the site of Fort Pownal to the lighthouse.

0.3 Walk along the shore, atop a steep drop to a side trail down to the shore.

0.6 The trail passes several picnic sites to a pier.

0.7 Walk uphill away from the pier to a parking area. Turn left onto a trail into the woods.

0.8 The trail ends at the road. Turn left and follow the road to the trailhead.

0.9 Arrive back at the trailhead.

Hike Index

About the Author

Greg Westrich grew up in Cincinnati and cut his hiking teeth in the Smoky Mountains and Kentucky's Red River Gorge. He has published more than forty articles in newspapers and magazines, and he is the author of *Hiking Maine* (FalconGuides). Greg and his wife, Ann, live in Glenburn, Maine, with their two children, Henry and Emma.

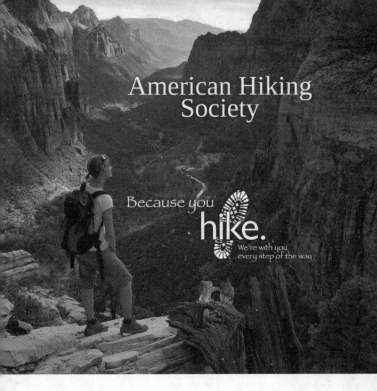

American Hiking Society

Because you hike.

We're with you every step of the way

As a national voice for hikers, **American Hiking Society** works every day:

- Building and maintaining hiking trails
- Educating and supporting hikers by providing information and resources
- Supporting hiking and trail organizations nationwide
- Speaking for hikers in the halls of Congress and with federal land managers

Whether you're a casual hiker or a seasoned backpacker, become a member of American Hiking Society and join the national hiking community! You'll enjoy great member benefits and help preserve the nation's hiking trails, so tomorrow's hike is even better than today's. We invite you to join us now!

American Hiking Society

www.AmericanHiking.org • info@AmericanHiking.org